Respectful Relationships and Effective Teaching

Understanding Challenging Behaviors of Persons with Disabilities

Larry Douglass

◆◆◆

Foreword by Nancy Weiss
Executive Director
TASH

Training Resource Network, Inc. ◆ St. Augustine, Florida

First Edition

This publication is sold with the understanding that the publisher is not engaged in rendering legal, financial, medical, or other such services. If legal advice or other such expert assistance is required, a competent professional in the appropriate field should be sought. All brand and product names are trademarks or registered trademarks of their respective companies.

Published by Training Resource Network, Inc., PO Box 439, St. Augustine, FL 32085-0439. You may order direct from the publisher for $24.95 plus $4.00 shipping by calling 800-280-7010 or visiting our website at www.trninc.com.

Printed in the United States of America by Sheridan Books on acid-free paper.

Library of Congress Cataloging-in-Publication Data

Douglass, Larry W., date.
    Respectful relationships and effective : understanding challenging behaviors of persons with disabilities / Larry Douglass.--1st ed.
        p. cm.
    Includes bibliographical references.
    ISBN 1-883302-54-4
    1. Children with mental disabilities--Education. 2. Children with mental disabilities--Behavior modification. 3. Effective teaching. 4. Teacher-student relationships. 5. Communication in education. I. Title.

LC4601.D68 2005
371.92--dc22

                                                                    2005043089

Jane—

11.4.05

You hold the only UK copy of the book and that's the way it should be. Thanks for helping Mary & I get off to the 'right' start here in Plymouth. We both owe you a great deal for taking us under your wing at Ridgeway... Hope you enjoy reading about my passion for teaching

I would like to dedicate this book to Mary Hoskin (my spouse) and Katherine Hoskin (Mary's mom). It was during Katie's year of illness prior to her death in 2003 that Mary and Katie's lives together humanized the universal message of the book. As Katie's illness worsened, words became less effective while their interdependence hinged on the reciprocal actions in their lives. Their time together created a natural staging of the book and its intended message. Their entire focus was ensuring their actions communicated the love and respect they held for each other. Much love and thanks to you both.

children.

Larry

◆

TABLE OF CONTENTS
◆◆◆

APPENDIX
LISTS OF POSSIBLE COMMUNICATIVE INTENT

ACKNOWLEDGEMENTS
♦♦♦

The value of this text belongs to the people I have had the pleasure of working with over the past thirty years. It would be my hope that those who read and enjoy its contents do so without seeing it as a book about disability, for it is a book about anyone with challenges. But for all of us who work and live with other people, we should understand that we will face behavioral challenges in life that will cause each of us to seek resolution for ourselves and others. So allow the text to speak to the broader issues of human behavior and I will feel I have done the *right thing* in writing the text.

Of course, there are many people to whom I credit any sensible and sensitive views I may hold in viewing the actions of others as meaningful and worthy. I have had great mentors–most of whom were my *students and/or learners*. Their numbers are uncountable. Concurrently, I do hold my professional and personal relationships with Lou Brown, Anne Donnellan, Wade Hitzing, Martha Leary, Herb Lovett, John McGee, John O'Brien, Jeff Strully, and Nancy Weiss as prerequisite to my being able to see the humanity in what I have chosen to do since the 1970s. Each of these friends has played a critical role in my success as an educator and as a human being entrusted with the learning of others.

I would also like to thank Anne, Dale, Gerry, Jack, Jeff, John, Julie, Kelli, Mary, Nancy, Paula, Quique, Rona, Susan, and Teddy for reading the original manuscript and for encouraging me to continue the project through its completion. And lastly, I need to thank a group of professional staff from Solano County, California, for their part in the Appendix.

♦

LARRY DOUGLASS
5, CORNERSTONE COURT
ROWE STREET
TORPOINT, CORNWALL
UK PL11 2LA
LARRYDOUGLASS@YAHOO.COM

FOREWORD
◆◆◆

NANCY R. WEISS, MSW
EXECUTIVE DIRECTOR, TASH

The best ways to support people with disabilities who have dangerous or disruptive behaviors is a hot topic of discussion among parents, teachers, and other professionals and advocates. Rarely, however, does one come across a book that offers truly new ways of thinking about supporting the people who most challenge us. This volume by Larry Douglass does just that.

In *Respectful Relationships and Effective Teaching* Douglass introduces us to students whom he describes as having "reputations that have a life of their own." He encourages us to strive to view their behaviors and motivations from their perspectives rather than from our own. He asks us to face our own motivations head-on: are we present in the lives of others to listen and support, or to control and coerce? He urges us not to build walls between ourselves and the people we support, but rather to engage them, build relationships, and allow them to serve as both students and teachers as we mutually seek lives of greater satisfaction and meaning.

Douglass calls upon all of us to re-evaluate our assumptions and the way we act upon those assumptions. He comes to the ideas presented in this book through his work as a classroom teacher and an advocate for his students for the past thirty years. He does not view his students and their difficult behaviors from afar, designing complex programs that, according to the books, should work. Rather he is with his students, side-by-side, discovering together the paths to better lives. Douglass refers to himself as a behavioral educationalist–a term he has coined and that he'll readily admit may have little meaning to others, but as you'll come to see, is a descriptor that is a good fit for the uncommon ways he approaches the challenges his students bring to him.

Throughout this text, Douglass cautions the reader about the seductive nature of traditional behavioral science – it is tempting to believe that human behavior, and therefore, behavior change, might work in scientifically predictable ways. He reminds us that if this is a science at all, it is one that is dependent on far too many variables to lend itself to "if she does 'A', and I do 'B', then she'll do 'C'" kind of thinking. Traditional behavior modification methods are enticing because they seem so logical and clean, while at the same time, serving to get us off the hook of having to really understand the person we are supporting from a perspective that often differs greatly from our own.

As Douglass points out so well, however, it is exactly that separation (between "supporter" and "supportee") that is inherent in traditional methods, which will result in those approaches being less successful over the long haul. Douglass warns, "by holding onto the mythology of the behavioral sciences, we can maintain our beliefs that individuals are solely responsible for their actions and challenges" (p. 30). We can continue to assure ourselves that they are the ones who are broken and need to be fixed – that it is not we who have to change our behaviors in their support. No one would argue that traditional methods of reinforcement or punishment can result in behavior change in the short term. But if our goal is to support real change and to give people tools that they can use to improve their success and impact for a lifetime, traditional techniques will never measure up to the kind of relationship-building and understanding that Douglass urges us to pursue.

A significant portion of what are viewed as inherent behavior problems are, in fact, people's efforts to protest the amount of control to which they are routinely subjected. Douglass introduces us to Dennis, a young man who refuses to wear shoes in school. Various overly simplified approaches to convincing Dennis to conform to conventional standards of footwear were not working – it was not until Dennis' actions were heard as the protest that they were, that Dennis was able to put down his picket sign and choose to keep his shoes on. If a person is acting in difficult ways in an attempt to make his or her voice heard, layering additional controls in an effort to change behavior is not only ineffective, but surely illogical as well.

The sad reality is, if you boiled down most behavior programs being implemented today in schools, group homes, and other program settings to their very essence, you'd arrive at something akin to the staff person, parent, or teacher saying (through his or her actions), "I'm in charge and you're not." If a person is behaving in challenging ways in response to the limitations of power and control that we often impose, creating programs that simply drive home those limitations seems self-defeating. The messages we communicate through our behavioral support should be much more in line with:

- I understand you
- I value and enjoy you
- I care about you
- I hear what you are conveying through your actions.

Whenever one person is trying to change the behavior of another, there is an inherent and unavoidable imbalance of power. While power imbalances may be inevitable – especially when we are talking about teacher-student or parent-child relationships, the "I'm in charge and you're not" message should be a subtle and unfortunate byproduct of any behavior change approach – not an end in itself.

Methods that rely on punishment are a perfect example of behavior change gone awry. Douglass speaks about the "real lesson" learned by children forced into timeout rooms the size of refrigerator boxes in Columbus, Ohio, schools in the late 1980s. He tells us that the lessons learned by the children were: that they are bad, that life is unpredictable, and that adults are cruel and manipulative (and lest we convince ourselves that such approaches are a thing of the past, look up "time out room" on the internet for a host of articles about schools still using this technique). As Douglass so aptly points out, punishment "applies a temporary patch, deafening the communication, only to have the message emerge in the form of another behavior," (p. 71) and predictably, an even more explosive or difficult behavior. If our goal is to assure the people with whom we work that they are valued, respected, and heard, punishment has no place in the behavior change toolbox.

The list of possible functions for different behaviors that Douglass provides starting on page 83 is excellent. Even if it does not list every possible idiosyncratic function that might be operating for any given individual, the list stimulates us to open our thinking in creative ways. Almost without exception, when I ask a person's team why they think that the individual might be behaving in certain ways, I receive one of two responses. The first is, "because he's non-compliant." Being non-compliant is a sin reserved for people with disabilities. What it really means is that this person is refusing to accept that we've got the power and he or she does not. Most negative descriptors have a corresponding positive descriptor, for example, "he's unfriendly/she's friendly" or "she's unproductive/he's productive". But have you ever heard someone say, "Oh, I met the nicest guy the other night ... and he's so compliant!" Or even, "I have three great kids – they are smart, funny, and wonderfully compliant!" It's not a goal we strive for, or call upon anyone else to strive for, except the people with disabilities we support.

The other function people think of when asked to hypothesize about the purpose difficult behaviors may serve, is that the person is acting that way "for attention." This is usually said in a tone that implies that there could be no greater transgression than to be acting out for attention. It escapes most people that there are few sadder realizations than that the only way someone can get the attention and recognition we all desire is to act in dramatically difficult ways. Our goal should be to assure the people we support that they will be valued and recognized without having to behave in ways that can't be ignored.

Throughout this volume, Douglass refers often to the work of the late Herb Lovett. Douglass gives the disability community a gift by continuing to speak in a voice that carries forth the original and treasured views that Lovett conveyed to us through his work and writings. A particular notion Lovett and I discussed kept returning to mind as I read Douglass' book for the first time. Lovett told me once that he urged teachers, psychologists, and behavior specialists to imagine that when they get to the pearly gates, every person for whom they had ever designed a behavior program will be lined up to welcome them. The goal, he would explain, is simply to do your work in such a way that when you encounter that line of folks, a far greater number would be motivated to step up, shake your hand, and thank you for making their lives better, than would the number who want nothing more than to haul off and slug you in the jaw. Lovett in his indomitable way was urging us to remember that while we're never going to get it right every time, our goal is not to overpower and control, but to offer people life changes that make sense to them and that they will continue to value over time. As Douglass reminds us, it would add grace to both people's lives if the battle for control were put aside in favor of more loving and life-affirming exchanges.

People with seriously difficult behaviors act not out of choice (or, as is sometimes assumed, to make the lives of their parents, teachers, and staff more difficult) but because some need is unmet for them. People act in challenging ways in an effort to assert control, achieve something that is desired, or obtain something held beyond their grasp. Douglass urges us to see value in this defiance. If we are willing to listen, sometimes the actions of the people we support provide the best evaluation of the quality of our services that we are ever going to receive. Behaviors change when we address the causes (the environment and demands) and when we help people to have better lives, rather than when we direct our attention to the symptoms (the behaviors). Good behavior supports are therefore proactive – they focus on what can be done to ensure that people do not need to exhibit difficult behaviors to achieve their needs. As Douglass conveys so well, building relationships and connections is the very foundation of this process.

Douglass reminds us that most of us would resist having a behavior program designed and applied to our own failings. Even positive behavioral approaches can be coercive and intrusive. A wise person who has a developmental disability once said, "I've got it figured out now. You better not tell them what you like, or they'll make you earn it -- and you better not tell them what you don't like or they'll use it against you" (Henning, 1991, lecture). When the focus stays on relationships and support, rather than on control and power, such risks are avoided. When people change their behaviors because their life experience has improved and they have less need to protest, these changes become part of their fabric, and everyone has cause for celebration.

Douglass recognizes that the first step of any successful behavior change approach is to understand the meaning of the behavior from the person's point of view. He introduces us to Ellen whose team insisted on understanding her difficult behavior of "sliming," or touching others with saliva on her hands, from their perspective instead of hers. He says of her team, "They simply could not take off their old glasses and don a new pair." (p. 11). Douglass emphasizes that until you can understand the meaning of a behavior for the person performing it, any attempt at behavior change is unlikely to be successful.

Sometimes when I speak with groups about the myriad of misguided ways in which we try to control people and their behaviors – and alternate ways that are not only humane but life-improving – someone will come up to me afterward with a question along the lines of, "I liked what you were saying, but what would you do about spitting?" and will go on to tell me a story about someone's behavior, intended to be truly horrifying. I assure them that if it were as easy as looking up spitting under "S" in a file drawer, we all would have figured this out a long time ago.

Douglass knows what to do about spitting (and the countless other behaviors which can be difficult, disruptive, dangerous, or self-destructive) and he brings his knowledge to the reader beautifully in this volume. Douglass does not urge us to accept all the people we support just as they are (and act) to the exclusion of supporting them to change behaviors that are difficult for them and others. Anyone who has worked in the real world, with real students and adults with disabilities, knows that people have behaviors that stand in the way of a better life – a life defined by connection with others and time spent doing things that are meaningful. Douglass urges us to give up on the notion that human reactions are as predictable as chemical reactions, and to accept that the very core of the behavior change process is in two people forming a relationship built on predictability and trust.

This idea – that solid, effective behavior change begins with something as familiar as building relationships – may represent such a departure from what we thought we knew that we are tempted to reject it. In fact it may seem like far too simple a notion compared to all the science and jargon of traditional behavior science. Often the ideas of divergent thinkers are rejected at first. Darwin's theories were ridiculed; it was clear that the Wright brothers would never get that machine off the ground – and when Copernicus espoused that it is the sun, not the earth, that is at the center of the universe, religious and secular leaders alike scorned his theory. Anyone could look up at the sky and confirm that it is the sun and moon that move in arcs around us, while we on earth sit firmly anchored in the center.

In *Respectful Relationships and Effective Teaching*, Douglass takes a page from Copernicus' songbook. What if we as teachers, parents, and professionals were able, as Douglass urges us, to truly accept that it is not all of us at the center of the behavior-change universe, but, rather, the people we support? It may be an uncomfortable notion because there is an urge to re-invent people in our own image – we were so sure that our task was to get the people we support to think and act more like us. What if we were wrong? Douglass' Copernicus-influenced view challenges us to make a fundamental shift and acknowledge that to assist people to accomplish real and meaningful change it is they who need to take their position in the center of their own universe. Our job, while often complex and uncertain, is only to help them assume their rightful place at the hub, and to support their discovery of their own power that awaits them there.

Nancy Weiss is the Executive Director of TASH, an international membership association devoted to equity, quality, and social justice for people with disabilities and their families. In a former life she ran a natural-setting positive behavioral support program for children and adults with severe disabilities. She can be reached at nweiss@tash.org. For more information about TASH go to www.tash.org.

Respectful Relationships and Effective Teaching

Understanding Challenging Behaviors of Persons with Disabilities

◆◆◆

CHAPTER ONE
♦♦♦

Ellen's Story

This book is built on the stories of many individuals and their families, who were treated poorly by the system but maintained their individuality despite their struggles. Let us begin with the first of many stories that capture the essence of the overwhelming need as well as a new direction. This story unfolds a new way to view behavior and starts the process of asking us in the field to undergo ethically based changes.

Misunderstanding Ellen

I had been working in the local high school as a special education teacher for about three years when I was required to have an individual educational plan (IEP) meeting for one of my students.

Ellen was a young woman I had known for many years, even at home with her parents prior to starting my teaching position at the high school. Ellen was full of impatience and frustration due to the nature of her intellectual disability and her inability to use words to communicate efficiently. Throughout her K-8 schooling, Ellen was consistently identified by her teachers and school staff as having serious behavior challenges.

In many ways, Ellen's reputation had a life of its own. It often was compiled of perceptions rather than actual understandings. She was a determined young woman who clearly enjoyed the social benefits of being in school while struggling to create relationships that left her in a positive light with adults. She continuously strove to communicate her needs and wants through hand gestures and non-verbal behaviors, although these messages were often misunderstood and ignored.

Throughout her schooling years, Ellen sought control whenever she thought her wishes were misunderstood or ignored. These moments of control took on a mild to desperate complexity depending on the nature of the situation. Many people labeled her as "aggressive," although "assertive" would be a better label for her actions in the face of her frustration and lack of control over events and situations.

Ellen's reputation accompanied her to high school. Her first few weeks were traumatic ones for everyone. In all honesty, I was hired following those initial weeks because the system started to recognize Ellen's extreme needs and challenges.

Regarding the IEP meeting, it seemed Ellen had been "sliming" people who taught and attended her adaptive physical education class. Let me explain what "sliming" means. Ellen would remove saliva and/or mucous from her mouth onto her fingers then wipe it on someone else's body, be it their arm or face. In today's schools, bodily fluids have been raised to only a fraction less of a concern than a bomb threat.

A team of people, including "professionals" and Ellen's dad, met one spring morning to write a behavior plan. I opened the meeting with a statement of the intent of Ellen's sliming. Following over two hours of discussion, the plan that was implemented and signed into the IEP was as follows:

> *If Ellen puts saliva/mucous on her fingers, the adult with her is to take out an antiseptic wipe and wash Ellen's hand immediately. This can also be done at a sink if one is readily available.*
>
> *As soon as Ellen is clean, she will be allowed to be close to others again.*
>
> *If Ellen successfully wipes the saliva/mucous on another, the same antiseptic wipe or sink will be used with the added requirement that Ellen approach the wronged individual to sign "sorry" for her actions.*
>
> *People can try to offer "high fives" to the clean hand only. (High fives had become less popular once everyone realized that Ellen's hands would oftentimes be unclean.)*

I tell this story because of its absolute disregard for Ellen's clear communicative intent through "sliming." In addition, let's review the plan based on the behavioral principles that were seemingly ignored by everyone, including two school psychologists at the meeting. This will unveil some of the myths and wrongs about approaching behavioral issues in this manner. Everyone felt this plan would be effective because:

1. the routine of making amends must be punishing to Ellen in order to bring about a reduction in her sliming behavior
2. the routine of apologizing for her wrongs would bring some form of understanding to Ellen that she did not have before the plan was created and implemented – in this case, the impact her behavior might be having on another individual and her role as the person who provides some explanation and/or apology to the person who has been wronged
3. the routine of cleansing her hands would bring some form of understanding to Ellen that she did not have before the plan was created and implemented – in this case, the danger of her germs and the possibility of spreading her germs to another individual.

From the point of behavior modification, we must look at only those possible explanations for the team's actions as they set out to write a plan that would reduce the occurrence of negative behavior. The three above descriptions do just that and only that. This investment in behavior management through the "science" of human behavior is significantly flawed and provides an uncountable number of pitfalls.

Let's go back and examine more of the story.

I had tried to tell the adults in Ellen's adaptive physical education class that the plan might simply be "feeding into" Ellen's actions and that Ellen's attention meter might be swinging high into the "red."

What was needed was to discover a possible "motivation" for this behavioral issue. An example of a tool to uncover this is Durand and Crimmins' *Motivation Assessment Scale*[1]. They worked out a very simple form for better understanding an individual's behavioral challenges. They designed the form to assist support staff through understanding the motivation behind an individual's challenges. They included four motivators in the form, asking support staff to focus on prepared questions.

Durand and Crimmins defined the four possibilities as:

1) sensory
2) escape/avoidance
3) attention
4) tangible

Answering and scoring the questions would result in a highest scoring motivator. The purpose of the form is to identify the motivator. The form is not designed to suggest interventions.

Yet, without analyzing motivation, Ellen's team seemed ready to make decisions to create a plan designed to reduce the identified behavior. Establishing behavior management plans without even investigating the behavioral motivation is absolutely flawed.

This behavior was, in fact, a game Ellen played very successfully. I tried to explain that many of our students are light-hearted and played games. However, it might be that Ellen's choice of games was not a good one. From Ellen's perspective, this game worked well and satisfied her definition of game playing. On the other hand, I knew the game had only one function, to satisfy Ellen. It was not a game of turn taking and reciprocity.

In many ways, it was not unlike many of the games Ellen had brought with her to high school. I then suggested that one sure way to overcome the "sliming" was to open up a wider variety of games for Ellen to play. Some of us had done that for Ellen throughout her high school years with great success. It was only this class that was plagued by this game.

But despite my best efforts, these ideas were dismissed. In hopes of making my point more concretely, I talked specifically about one such game we played with Ellen. I told them when Ellen touched her nose, I responded by touching her nose. She would then touch her chin and I would respond in kind. This playfulness would then be repeated until one of us finally tired, usually me.

I am not sure if they heard a single word about Ellen's playfulness, but I do know that the team latched onto the specificity of the "game" I was describing. Immediately, the "age-inappropriate" nature of this game became the focus of our discussion.

Their concern centered totally around the issue of an eighteen-year-old young woman's playing a "game" of touching noses with an adult. Their issue was that this "game" might be appropriate for a young child, but not for a young woman. The issue of age-appropriate has long been a divisive topic within our field and was the "red flag" for the people sitting around the table discussing Ellen's issues.

I was thinking throughout this tangential discussion about our being located on a high school campus where touching was the norm amongst students. True, touching noses was not commonly witnessed, but touching was pervasive.

The meeting proceeded with a highly negative discussion about this specific game. I assured them it fit the definition of a healthy game since both Ellen and I had roles and parts to play.

One opposing teacher suggested that "high five" would be a better game. He stated that whenever he offered her a high five for doing good work, Ellen seemed pleased and responded by putting her hand into the air. I mentioned that in that particular example, the high five was not a game. It was actually reinforcement for satisfying this educator's expectations.

How clearly this confirmed the differences between acting on someone's communicative intent and acting within the science of behavior modification. The team member had introduced the "high five" as if it were a playful choice Ellen would have made. He offered Ellen the "high five" as a contingent reward for what Ellen did to satisfy his expectations.

This is where we cannot straddle the fence. If we are looking at Ellen's actions as playful, we cannot redefine this "high five" sequence as being playful. It is entirely different and needs to be kept totally separate. You can award someone a "high five" without any recognition of that individual's efforts to create a meaningful message through his or her actions. We always should be clear which glasses we use when we focus on another's behavior. Don't cheat. Don't fudge. Be honest.

It might be easy to see something like "high five" as a playful act happening between two individuals (team members on a sports team), but it is imperative to identify most "high fives" as a reward for behavior that is pleasing to another. More specifically, "high five" is a reinforcing message designed to let a person know you are in favor of their behavior. It is not a game played between individuals. We see "high fives" being given as one student returns to their seat after doing well on a spelling bee, or after one player scores for their team, or after an individual has won eight tether ball matches before being defeated.

Knowing the meaning of your personal contact with another is critical in understanding whether we are being "playful" or "rewarding." When we offer a reward, we seek to reinforce another's behavior and, thereby, let them know we want to see more of that particular behavior or action.

When we are being playful, in hopes of responding to another's request for a playful relationship, we are not seeking to reinforce any particular action by an individual. We simply are providing a reciprocal action that can and will maintain the playfulness of our relationship or game.

Ellen's team, I felt, had some serious misconceptions regarding Ellen's behavior, as well as disregard for Ellen and her actions as meaningful and sophisticated. The other team members plowed ahead as if I had spoken a foreign language. The team faced a moral crisis. Unfortunately, they did not see the difference between what Ellen had taught us about her life and her ability to tell jokes. Ellen, as an individual with significant intellectual difficulties, could not be credited with an accomplishment such as telling jokes and making up games that can be played with another human being.

As the meeting ended, I knew that we had created a document that:
  1) would provide them absolutely no relief from the dreaded sliming
  2) might even bring about an increase in the behavior.

I would not allow this to impact my relationship with Ellen and her abilities to be a "stand up" comedian and a person of mirth rather than a person of germs. In closing Ellen's story, I want to assure you that my job did not change because of that plan. I continued to find the jokes in Ellen's messages and actions. I tried to open others up to her humor while shaping her jokes so they would be more recognizable.

Seeing Ellen through New Glasses

Let's now review Ellen's situation in a more functional way – a communicative way!

Taking a History and Reputation
and Building a Relationship

I had been Ellen's teacher for almost three years by the date of the meeting to develop a behavior plan. I also had been fortunate enough to have known Ellen both in her home and her pre-high-school settings. When she entered the high school, she came with all her flare and flamboyance.

I was hired soon thereafter because the high school was not doing well with Ellen and one other graduate from the K-8 system. With my history and knowledge of Ellen, I tried to create a positive path for her high school education. I set up campus jobs and experiences with other high school girls. I tried to learn as much as I could about Ellen's inner most ways.

She had lived on thin ice for her entire K-8 years as people tried to behaviorally modify her to become their version of a model citizen. They were constantly changing her school routine, removing privileges, and imposing fines for her many wrongs. They gave her things she said she wanted and took them away in the next breath in order to punish her for negative behavior.

In fact, Ellen entered high school displaying her master's degree in human manipulation – a skill she had learned and perfected along the way. She needed it in order to survive her educators de jour. She had learned far more than any of her teachers were willing to acknowledge. They would not want to take credit for teaching her, for example, that she would have to hit someone to get them to pay attention to her needs and wants.

Nor would they acknowledge teaching her to save a little urine for a time later in the day when she might need to bring things to a standstill. She was (and still is) savvy and wise. As we set about untangling the kinks, I discovered the person I grew to cherish as a strong and determined young woman.

I also encountered many of Ellen's challenges along that path. I was struck, bitten, and slimed, as well as charmed by her personality. Since I use only one "lens" when I try to understand an individual's behavior, I was steadfast in my determination to move away from the labels: aggressive, angry, selfish, hurtful, unclean, etc., and into a new arena where we read Ellen's actions as meaningful language. Ellen could tell us about her life with signs. She could tell us about her personal self and her previous school life if we could just listen to her actions and use the right tool to decipher her messages.

Being obstinate, I was determined to listen properly without judging her actions as they were previously labeled. I quickly noticed that sometimes when I was hit, Ellen was not really angry about anything. It was also apparent the "blow" had a gentler tone to it. Now, if you are looking for messages in actions, here's a window of opportunity. It was very clear to me that if we defined our relationship with Ellen built on honesty and interdependence we might witness Ellen communicating her intentions and needs.

For three years, Ellen and I tried quite successfully to work around difficult situations and to work through them if the need arose. We had a very strong relationship that could be elastic if it needed to be. So for over three years Ellen taught and learned. And for two years, we also learned and taught – interdependence at its finest.

Discovering the Hidden Comedian

By the time Ellen's comedic personality started to become clear, we had successfully worked our way through many of the challenges Ellen had brought to high school.

For example, wearing shoes was a major challenge for Ellen in her K-8 years. Despite many efforts, this behavior remained a difficulty. But in high school, Ellen wore her shoes throughout the school day. It was like seeing her say, "I need my shoes 'cause we have places to go and people to see."

Now that we had a new relationship based on trust and honesty, it was time to make sense of Ellen's hitting. If she wasn't mad, what was she trying to express? Hoping to find the best qualities in an individual, I headed to the "game theory" for hitting. For months following, Ellen would hit me and I would tap her back. We would play the "harder to softer" tap game.

It was wonderful because it gave Ellen a chance to play her game without the roof falling in on her. She never faced a punishing consequence for any of her hitting and got a playful response if it was within our reach. I say that because we are not always able emotionally to give that extra bit when it is so needed. So, we did our best. That's all anyone can ask for!

It was a delight to get the call from Ellen to play the hitting game. She would always start out harder than I would, but the joy came as we worked our way through the levels of firmness to softness as the game played out. With this new understanding of Ellen, I was becoming more acutely aware of her vulnerability and limited skills in this funny, unique game-playing area. But if she could be playful in hitting, she could be that person in other ways too.

The Nose Game

Ellen and I became helpers and friends to some of the girls who attended the girls' varsity basketball practice PE class. At first just interested spectators, we started to take on more of a presence during this daily event. We established routines and carried out chores. Ellen thought it was terrific to be part of something special at the school. She eagerly attended home games and traveled to the state tournament.

Basketball was Ellen and Ellen was basketball. But like most of the girls in the class, she was not always actively engaged. Ellen introduced her new "game" to me, to the coach, and to many of the basketball players. She would touch her nose and we would reciprocate. It was easy, it was safe, it was gentle and it was based on trust. We were on an even better path. It did not originate from an old hitting habit. It did not need reworking. It just needed playing.

So for hours and weeks and months, I would answer Ellen's request to play. Anyone, after a simple – "She wants you to touch her nose" – could play this game with Ellen. And they did. They weren't ashamed to have been taught a turn-taking game by Ellen. They were delighted.

All I was trying to explain to the other professional members of Ellen's IEP team was that this sliming behavior that was plaguing them was nothing more or less than a request from Ellen to play with them. I would have been the first to agree that given the present nature of the game, it should not be played at face value. Like hitting, it would require some adjustments.

But following the adjustments, everyone would have a game to play with Ellen. Regardless of my attempted salesmanship, the team failed to see Ellen as a joke teller and game player. They simply could not take off their old glasses and don a new pair.

Ellen was ready to play, but she had no partners. In all the jargon babble, the team lost a golden opportunity to make a real change. I could only wonder why people get so locked into the technology and jargon that they are unavailable to see what the actions of another might be saying.

It is critical to digress at this point to discuss further the communicative intent of behavior. As highlighted in many of the above interpretations of Ellen's behavioral challenges, each understanding came through the lens of reading and listening to the non-verbal messages in another's actions. From that moment on, we have one and only one mission – to understand the message and to honor its value to the person.

I am by no means the first person to claim and name this process, but it is a process I believe promotes fundamental changes in the human relationships that exist between a parent and child, between a teacher and student, and between a professional human services staff and client.

The notion of communicative intent has been around for well over a decade through for the work of many, including Anne Donnellan and Richard Mesaros. Even with the ever increasing ways of understanding the actions of others, I still find the term appropriate for use today. For, as a term, communicative intent creates no barriers and creates no limits to our vision and creativity. But to see communicative intent as a definer of behavior, one must throw away the old way of viewing an individual's actions. It is virtually impossible to see traditional behavior modification as a possibility through the lenses of "communicative intent."

Likewise, it is virtually impossible to use communicative intent to guide you when you are wearing the glasses of a behavior modifier. It is always important to define your motivation when you offer guidance to another. The question you must face head-on is whether you are really present in someone's life to listen or you are there really to coerce. When you are there to listen, you can act only on what you hear, be they words or actions. You cannot judge the actions as worthy of the science of behavior modification.

If you hear another's message, you must be honest to both the person and his or her message. And when it comes to offering guidance, you can suggest that their means of telling their story is sometimes difficult to hear. You can suggest ways they can relay their message more softly, more gently, and in a more friendly way.

Listening is an art, not an intervention. Listening takes into account the human trust that should exist in all our relationships. Through communicative intent, we limit our focus to listening without judgment. It is a change that is necessary and essential to bettering our lives as well as the lives of others.

On the other hand, we also must understand the impersonal nature of the sciences that some say define humans and their actions. These types of interventions are not based on listening to the messages of others. On the contrary, the sciences are used as tools to manipulate and control the actions of others and their access to community and inclusion. There is a fundamental distinction between the one who listens to another person and the one who coerces another person. These distinctions, above all else, define the direction of this book.

By thinking behavior modification can be slightly skewed into true behavioral support for an individual, we are gravely ill-informed and potentially dangerous to the person whom we profess to be guiding.

I must include just a few more thoughts about Ellen before closing this chapter. When I referred to Ellen as a comedian, I meant that as something beyond just the games she would create and play. Most striking was a joke she would tell by pointing to the floor. We started out trying hard to figure out just what that action might be saying. We asked Ellen questions and struggled to reveal its communicative intent, but we never came to a satisfactory answer.

Then we realized that on a rare occasion in this school, but probably much more frequently in her previous schools, Ellen would spite everyone by voiding on the floor after she had sat down. We decided to view her pointing as this message: "I could go to the bathroom on that spot, if I wanted." Now that's going out on a limb, but it made as much sense as anything else and supported Ellen as a joke teller. So from that time on, we would smile and laugh with her when she pointed to the ground. I chose to step on the spot. That gave me an action to do that might be saying, "I stamped out that spot. That's funny." Sometimes, others would point to another spot as the exchange got funnier and crazier. Needless to say, Ellen never defined the message of her actions. She did not have to; it was a JOKE!

[1]V. Mark Durand and Daniel B. Crimmins, *The Motivation Assessment Scale (MAS): Administration Guide,* Topeka, Kansas: Monaco and Associates, 1992

CHAPTER TWO

◆◆◆

Reconsidering the Science of Human Behavior

"If Pavlov and Skinner had been working with cats rather than dogs and pigeons, behaviorism would have never been born. And I think humans act more like cats."

– Mary Poplin

Based on the works of hundreds, if not thousands, of behavioral researchers, we have been taught to see human behavior as a sort of predictable phenomena. I do not disagree totally with the notion that human behavior is completely predictable. I simply doubt the idea that applying scientific technologies such as behavior management and behavior modification provides us with the only way to understand and address an individual's behavioral challenges.

My belief does not come from the core foci of behavior management and behavior modification, which directs us to design "programs" that reward or punish people based on what we know they prefer and dislike. My belief arises from the working knowledge that the science of human behavior can distort our vision of individuals and prevent us from seeing them as complex individuals with complex issues.

This book is about alternatives to the behavioral sciences to employ as we learn to question ourselves and our motivation while supporting individuals and their behavioral challenges. It is not about "what not to do," but rather, what you might do instead of establishing a behavior modification program for an individual you support or teach. For if we have learned anything in the past decade or so, we know that asking an individual with disabilities to make changes requires offering alternatives to current habits and behaviors. We know we need to work on the premise that this need for alternatives is just as relevant to teachers, parents, caregivers, and adult service staff. It is only through exploring these alternatives that we find replacement choices for our current practices and strategies.

I recall when the California Hughes Bill (a state nonaversive education law) passed in the early 1990s. It included well-written regulations that spelled out what educators where required to do on behalf of children with serious behavioral challenges. There were also a number of "don't dos" that typically left teachers thinking they had lost their tools without having replacement strategies. This was not the bill's intent, but it left educators bewildered about what was left for them to use in their attempts to support their most challenging students. Being told what not to do is never as valuable as being told what else you might try doing! This book offers alternatives to our more traditional behavioral approaches.

We have been taught to apply the principles of the behavioral sciences to glean a remedy when we assume that an individual is knowingly withholding a skill or behavior. When we do, we approach a solution without asking a myriad of questions that lie down a divergent path. We default to a behavior modification stance prematurely in many cases. The following example questions the use of the behavioral sciences in light of the possibility that our understanding is not complete.

Anne Donnellan, a well-known university faculty member and author of several books on behavior and autism, formerly from the University of Wisconsin/Madison, would often show a slide during her lectures of a black and white collage. She would then ask the audience, "Does anyone see a cow?" Remarkably, large numbers of people would respond positively to her query. Many others sat in bewilderment.

Anne would then show the same collage with additional magnification. She would repeat her question to the audience and more "seers" would join the ranks. But, there were always people who could not see the cow regardless of how hard they tried. Anne, hoping everyone could become a seer, would change the optical image in yet another way before repeating her question. As one who still could not see the cow, I was left sitting and wondering if it was all a joke or a hoax. But around me, people were claiming to have seen the cow.

I was feeling less than great when Anne asked those of us remaining, "If I gave you an M&M, could you see the cow? If I sent you to timeout, could you see the cow? If I shocked you with a cattle prod, could you see the cow?"

What a relief I felt when I realized that for some reason I simply could not optically arrange the splotches into a recognizable form. It is possible to believe that if Anne took a laser pointer and detailed the connection between the splotches, I could join the ranks of those who saw the image. But would that really teach me how to make my brain organize randomly arranged splotches into a recognizable image, or would it simply provide me a way to see this image at this moment?

And at that moment I also realized that I could not be behaviorally modified into seeing the cow. Sadly enough, I could be behaviorally modified into claiming to see the cow in order to get what was due me or to avoid what might happen. So the questions are, "Is it ethical to assume I was simply withholding my recognition of the image?" and "Is it ethical to assume I would produce the appropriate behavior under the promise of reward or the threat of punishment?"

Before opening up more crucial questions about the values and ethics behind behavior modification, let's look more globally at behavior management. While addressing a class of future teachers at California State University/Sacramento, I was describing in detail the need for a classroom management system. All societies, communities, and classrooms need an umbrella, or maybe a net, of rules and governing principles that maintain that grouping of individuals as a community.

I stressed that they need to choose such a system based on their exposure to the variety of different options and how they feel about those choices. The system individual educators might choose for their classrooms needs to feel good to each individual's ethics and values. If the chosen system feels right, the educator will make it ethically valued for the students. I went on to add that in today's America, you can expect that any classroom management system will not work well for about ten percent of the students.

The ten percent figure has come to be my marker for the two or three students within a classroom whose challenges go beyond the reach of a management system and traditional awards and takeaways. Throughout my years as a "behavioral consultant," I was routinely told about the two or three children within any class who did not make it under the teacher's community umbrella. Not long ago, I was asked by a general education teacher in Santa Barbara, California, "Is teaching going to get any easier or is the influx of behaviorally complicated students coming into general education here to stay?"

The answer I gave at that time still holds true today. "Today's children and young adults with disabilities are increasingly more behaviorally complex, more culturally complex, more linguistically complex, and more socially complex. They will continue to bring their complexities into our classroom, community residences, and places of employment for the foreseeable future." Maybe we don't want or don't like that answer, but I believe it is true. It needs to be addressed by every teacher and adult service staff in America. Again, the same is true in our work with adults with disabilities who need our support.

That leaves us to solve a very important quandary. How do we respond to the behavioral needs of a minority of the people we serve? One solution might be the historically acceptable path whereby we label those individuals as "noncompliant, deviant, unmotivated, unreachable, or possessing no conscience." This process lets us lay blame on them for their failure to "get with the program." Labeling individuals clearly separates them from the mainstream and ties the cause of their dysfunction to them. When we tie labeling and the behavioral sciences, we forego asking the most important questions before we design something to bring about a positive change for everyone.

Sadly enough, labeling and blaming has been an acceptable school and adult service strategy. But the act of blaming the individual for his or her behavioral inadequacies is not a positive path for the provider, the teacher, or the individual. I have visited many classrooms where I worked with many teachers in an attempt to help them see their student in a "different way." I have always been struck by how easily some educators, who are also parents, are able to distance themselves from their challenging students and their parents. The primary way educators are able to create this distance is through the labels they attach to both the children and their parents. They move people away by creating labels that demonize other adults, who also are struggling with the challenges of their children.

We need to constantly strive to avoid that distorted perspective regarding our students. It is important to remove the pair of glasses that limits us in our efforts to see others. We must proceed to don a new pair of glasses that provides a new vision for understanding the behavior of that ten percent. Shedding the technology of human behavior can be very difficult. At the same time, it can be very valuable to both the support person and the individual.

More often than I want to count, I have come across education and disability professionals whose limited knowledge of the behavioral sciences has frightened me. They could not see the individual with challenges beyond behavioral technology. On the other hand, I have seen hundreds of similar professionals embrace the possibilities that lie outside the behavioral sciences. That is the most encouraging aspect of working with people. You never can be sure who will make the leap and who will not.

It is my hope that this book will enhance the lives of those people you teach or support, particularly that ten percent. The information supplements any management system. More importantly, it gives you concrete strategies and information for helping those with the most needs. So don't fear losing your management systems. But be prepared to abandon many of those behavior modification tactics with which we have become all too familiar and comfortable.

An Understanding of What Limits Our Thinking

While testifying recently on behalf of a fourth grade boy with special education needs, I was convinced that the boy's ability to perform the sought-after skills was simply not in his repertoire. A fairly thorough behavior plan had been developed for this young boy, but it omitted all the components of teaching that the boy so desperately needed to acquire those sought-after skills.

As the plan was designed, the boy was to be rewarded and punished for the presence of the school's expected skills. The plan was not designed to teach the boy the skills. It was a behavior modification plan, not a teaching plan. I would have seen the plan in a very different light if it had:

1) outlined the needed skills
2) assessed their availability to the student
3) focused on how the skills could be taught in various settings
4) prescribed the teaching strategies for his educators.

Since the plan was written only to award and punish, the boy was blamed for willful acts based on the premise that he was choosing not to use his skills in the appropriate situations at the appropriate times. When a student is seen in that light, we are bound to make crucial errors in our analysis of his or her issues. We also are bound to overstretch the value and teaching potential of behavior modification. For when an individual finds himself or herself in an impossible situation based on his or her lack of skills, it is not a time to learn the skills, unless the teachers are prepared to teach to the need of the student.

When we make errors of this magnitude, we begin to fabricate an entire story and rationale for our treatment of a student. We begin acting on non-truths in the name of science. This is an error that we must be willing to shed as we move away from a behavior modification model, in search of understanding the communicative intent of a student's behaviors. The term communicative intent is the backbone of the strategies in this book. It is the direction I hope we can all travel together. If we looked at this boy's behaviors as communicative, we might think, for example, that he is unable to play cooperatively with his peers because he lacks

1) language to express his frustration
2) cooperative skills needed to play with others
3) ability to manage his anger when competing with another child
4) a neurological trigger for controlling his emotions
5) ability to step out of a difficult situation
6) basic ability to share and take turns with a peer.

If we look into questions of this nature rather than just investing in the technology of behavioral science, our understanding of this young boy would be the focus of our efforts. Once we understand the answers to these and similar questions, we can partner our efforts with the boy's needs. This is a positive alternative to the notion that positive or negative motivation will cause the boy to use skills he does not have in his repertoire.

In another example, let's investigate how the behavioral sciences can be helpful and challenge ourselves to look beyond the technology as we view the individual's behavioral challenges through these new lenses. I currently have a fifth grader in my class who has the label of autism. Many times when he joins us for breakfast he does not eat any of his food. I know that he comes to school without eating at home and he should be having breakfast along with my other students.

It would be possible to establish some form of "program" to get him to eat like my other students. We could set up a "You can't do ___ until you eat your breakfast" intervention. This clearly would be based on a behavioral sciences approach. We would expect his eventual realization that he must eat something before moving on in his day. But the "what ifs" underlying this situation are more important than establishing this type of program. Let's say that maybe:

1) he really isn't hungry
2) he is not a morning person
3) he is not well enough to eat
4) he hates all the food choices
5) he simply cannot make his body perform the needed motor movements to allow him to eat his breakfast.

Now we have begun to open up the possibilities for this young boy's issues around breakfast. But, let us be honest. We could have chosen the behavioral sciences approach without any consideration of possibilities such as those listed. Would we have been right to use behavior modification in this situation? Would we have actively listened to his actions? "Listening" is what we need to do as we experience the challenges others experience in their lives.

Before moving on, let's investigate another real life situation. The question is, "How would we think about a student who removes his shoes in school in what looks like an act of defiance?" I recently attended a series of three IEP meetings for a former student in which we discussed his refusal to wear his shoes. Dennis had just completed his fourth year in high school and was about to begin his second group of four years on the same campus. Dennis had come from an ill-matched K-8 system and was not allowed to attend a full day in school until his sophomore year.

For those long eight years in pubic school, Dennis had been the recipient of a shopping list of labels that included aggressive, severely retarded, hurtful, lazy, and primitive. He was granted only the minimal services and was allowed almost no access to a curriculum or interaction with others. He was deemed too needy for a quality education. He had almost no opportunity to anticipate regularity in his school routine or to see the school world as one that would bring both learning and enjoyment.

In high school, Dennis and I found ourselves looking back at the past with great disappointment. We looked to the future with an agreement that, despite our challenges, things were bound to change. So as Dennis' teacher, I participated with him in school life and we tried our best to be engaged and productive. Dennis' behavioral challenges were always an issue, but that was a given, so we pushed ahead. Given the possibility that Dennis did not see any reason to wear his shoes, I was set on providing both an education and a reason for his wearing his clothes and shoes while at school. Given that high school students are not allowed to be at school without their shoes, I couldn't see why Dennis should be the exception. What if we approached it from the point of view that Dennis had no idea what was available to him as a student in this new school?

I could have looked at Dennis' refusal to wear his shoes as his personal statement, "I do not want to wear shoes." I could have seen his refusal as the culmination of his analysis of the situation and its pertinence to his own desires and strengths. I could have relaxed and asked Dennis to tell me when he was ready to go by allowing me to put on his shoes. I could have also established a "you put on your shoes and we will do something special" attitude toward Dennis or even an, "I'm sorry, we cannot do ___ since you do not have on your shoes" attitude.

All these directions would have been accepted by my administration and by my teaching peers. It would have been defensible at the next IEP meeting on just those grounds, so why not? If we undertake a commitment to a rich school life and a consistent track, Dennis would learn that keeping on his shoes would provide places to go, people to see, commitments to keep, and a relationship to uphold.

Let's get back to the three IEP meetings to better understand what had changed for Dennis. We had spent almost seven hours discussing his schedule or lack of a schedule, his non-participation, their limited staffing, his unmet IEP goals, his seizures, his toileting issues, and his aggressive actions. Finally, somewhere in the middle of the third meeting, it was finally revealed that Dennis' education was governed by his not wearing his shoes. His new teachers had adopted the societal rule of NO SHOES – NO EDUCATION.

Now the truth was on the table and here is where the story saddens for me. The team had established a poorly written "behavior plan" that governed Dennis' entire school life. The plan was not designed to open doors for Dennis, but was designed to set contingencies on his school activities.

They had written a plan that said Dennis' mother would take him home if the school was unable to manage his challenges. It was a plan that focused on his medical issues and their inability to maintain him when he was most challenging. It mentioned his communication through his behaviors, but did not address possible messages that might be available if they were active listeners.

They were dangling Dennis' previously established full participation in school in front of him like a carrot. It was their goal to make Dennis earn back his previous education. The plan, though not officially written within an IEP meeting, clearly stated, "If he removes his shoes, he cannot leave the room and/ or he will be required to stop any activity until he is willing to have his shoes put back on his feet."

Dennis' education was being held hostage by their way of viewing his actions. His education was being strangled by a behavior modification plan.

In my view of teaching, there is an agreement between a student and educator that binds both parties to the provision of an education. But through their legal documents and actions, they were not engaged in this type of mutually reciprocal agreement.

In my understanding of the law, there exists no provision that empowers one party to hold an education beyond the grasp of another. But in the name of behavioral compliance, Dennis was denied what had been available to him during the first three years at this school. It was clear to Dennis, his mom, and me that we finally understood what was wrong with this picture. Not only had the team established a coercive protocol, they were denying Dennis access to the campus and to his established contacts.

The team announced that they were not making any progress in this effort, but they were willing to hang onto the failing plan for another school year if needed. The idea that a group would cling to a behavior plan that was not regaining lost ground for Dennis did not make any sense to either his mother or me.

Except for his mom's year-long struggle to get Dennis back to where he had been, no one advocated for Dennis. They simply wanted permission to continue the plan. No one could or would put into words the situation from Dennis' perspective. Though I was unable to promote Dennis' perspective at the meeting, let me take a stab at it now.

For Dennis, the message was clear, "I have no routines, no responsibilities to fulfill, no commitments to keep, no destinations to reach and guess what – no shoes, no socks, and no shirt – and the final kicker – no education and no worth." Dennis had not managed to get back his previous school schedule regardless of what he had been willing to contribute.

At times, Dennis gave it his best but surmised that things just were not going to happen. He had been taught, "Why believe in it?" For all those months of sitting and waiting for something to happen, Dennis' trust for his teachers and for his routines had eroded. It was bound to happen, because, like all of us, Dennis is human. He clearly saw the evaporation of his school experiences, his acquaintances, his travels, his jobs, his responsibilities, his beliefs, his trust, and his self-worth. After being a valued member of a high school campus and an active participant in school life, Dennis well understood that he no longer ranked as that valued individual.

Let's get back to the meeting and the plan. So here we were, fourteen months later, sitting around a table with a bevy of professionals talking about what Dennis had to do in regard to his shoes. The obligations of the professionals were not mentioned. Nothing was discussed regarding what they might need to do to repay Dennis for the destruction of his trust and school life.

Once again, for the sake of a tired and failed plan, no one could see Dennis, the young man, through the fog of behaviorism. No one made any mention of their role in either the destruction of his school life or what they felt obligated to do tomorrow to start the healing process. All they could see was the plan and Dennis' failure to play his role appropriately and willingly.

They explained to us that they had sat on the floor with Dennis to demonstrate, point blank, the outcome of wearing shoes. The aide and teacher removed their shoes and socks while they sat alongside Dennis. Then, they replaced their socks and shoes, stood up, collected their lunch boxes, and announced, "We are going to lunch because we have on our shoes and socks." They were invested in the idea that he had to perform correctly and appropriately in order to gain the "right" to go to lunch at an outside bench. For months by this time, Dennis had been eating his lunch in the classroom because he would not keep his shoes on his feet.

In contrast, Dennis had previously been able to enjoy his lunch amongst the entire high school student body, whether he ate in the cafeteria, outside on a bench, or in front of a rock band assembly perched on the hillside. Dennis knew of nothing else and had never been denied these opportunities that had made his high school experience different and valuable. But despite these considerations, Dennis was being managed unsuccessfully through a behavior plan that offered no escape for anyone. After all these months Dennis must have seen things from a very dismal perspective.

Was the team truly unaware of Dennis' understanding of the significance of wearing his shoes and socks? Did they really think he was going to yield to their display of control? Did they really believe that this was an exercise in restoring confidence and trust into a truly damaged relationship?

One might need to ask: Is the science and technology so enticing that we, as professionals, cannot see that the obstacles might be the plan in our fabricated vision of the individual?

As Dennis' advocate, I wanted to talk about these issues with his teaching staff. Seeing we had no place for any further discussion in this arena, his mother asked that they provide some information about their plan's effectiveness. We were willing to let them have four weeks to clearly define just how limiting their plan was and how much of an impact on Dennis' school experience his not wearing his shoes would prove to be. It was our hope that once they examined the substance or lack thereof in the plan, they would reconsider their chosen path for Dennis. We hoped that they would see that they had locked themselves into a form of singular vision and were trapped, as was Dennis. To prevent this quagmire, we cannot allow this behavioral form of control to guide our understanding of people and their behaviors.

Before closing this chapter, I would like to relate a story from Herb Lovett. Herb tried to create a way for people to think about how they view an individual and his or her challenges. He served as the conscience for the "behavior field" until his untimely death in 1998. Herb's commitment, in writings and in practice, was to first see the individual as a person. This has shaped his legacy.

I worked directly with Herb in many situations. I always was interested to watch his dismantling of the negatives of behaviorism and punishment in order to get the team, the family, the professional, and the system to see what we could learn through listening to the actions and words of another.

Herb received his doctorate in psychology in the 1980s and turned to both writing books (*Cognitive Counseling for Persons with Special Needs* and *Learning to Listen*) and consulting to convey his message to the field. He never underestimated the power of the human spirit and the humanity in what each of us brings to our social community. When he was confronted with the proverbial story about an individual with a disability whose challenges were about to be discussed openly in front of a group, Herb would tell a great story about people who had decided that overcorrection was the solution to what was more than likely a very complex human problem. For, by definition, overcorrection requires that an individual makes things "right" over and over again so that they might learn to avoid the behavior that got them into this punishing intervention. To avoid having to overcorrect one's errors, one should avoid using the behavior what was subject to the overcorrection.

Herb, as he always did, brought the issue right down to the human level. Herb did not question the correctness of the procedure. Rather, he questioned its humanity. What would happen, he asked, if you were visiting a friend for dinner and you spilled red wine on a white couch? Under any circumstances, would your host make you take the couch apart and clean it, on the spot and in front of everyone, and then make you put it all back together? And then make you take the couch apart again and clean it in front of everyone, and then put it all back together? And do it all again once more? As with the many stories Herb told, let this one be added to the list of one worth telling and retelling.

Herb's anecdote clearly demonstrates how humanity prevails when we are not behavioral scientists. Herb would go on to tell that you would offer to make amends, but your friend would thank you without accepting your offer. The host would relieve you of your guilt and assure you that the couch would be cleaned at a later time. You might even offer to pay for the cleaning, but your guest would assure you it would be taken care of and not to worry yourself any further. Both you and your host would go on to have an enjoyable evening of food, conversation, and companionship.

It hopefully would not be the last time you were ever invited over for dinner. That is what humans do on behalf of other humans whose company and relationship they cherish. Let us smile at the knowledge that there is always another way at looking at another human and their actions. Could Dennis' teacher succeed in seeing Dennis and his actions as human?

I can pass along the outcome of our last meeting with Dennis' teacher. It was remarkable how much change had happened for this person. I cannot account for the change, but I am more than happy to tell the story because we need to have hope that all of us can make positive changes on behalf of those we support. Within months, Dennis' teacher had seen him in a different light, for she spoke of getting him a job, taking him into the community, riding public transportation, working alongside him on being productive and valued and, most striking, doing all this without the behavior plan.

Maybe this promising ending to very long and drawn-out struggle will mark a change in direction for both Dennis and his teacher. It is stories like this one that show both the quicksand of behavior modification and the hope that comes when someone is able to see beyond the technology to find a person waiting to be heard and valued.

CHAPTER THREE
◆◆◆

A New Path:
Starting with the Possibilities

Change is a difficult process for anyone, not just individuals with labels and leaning challenges. We all have incredible learning needs when it comes to seeing behavior in a different way. Change can work its way into an individual's life only after the change process has started for us.

This is oftentimes a difficult place for workers in the field to go. We have been trained to see the problem as belonging to the individual with challenges. This type of training and perspective negatively influences our ability to be open to new possibilities. The transformation of responsibility and ownership must start with the professional, the parents, and the direct care staff before we ask others to join us in making changes in themselves that impact how they act.

Communicative Intent

First, let's review communicative intent. This is the bedrock for each and every move that follows as we work our way together through this text. Communicative intent simply attaches a non-verbal message to the actions of another. It is that basic.

When communicative intent first appeared in the literature in the 1980s, it was quite understandable. The research was directed at individuals with significant intellectual disabilities and significant verbal language challenges. Anne Donnellan, Richard Mesaros, and their colleagues designed a plotting format to identify what non-verbal means were used by an individual to express one or many feelings, needs, wants, or emotions.

Since this early research and its publication, we have seen an explosion of articles and books written by an array of noted authors from the fields of special education, positive behavioral support, and speech and language pathology. A literature search finds Edward Carr, Anne Donnellan, Mark Durand, Rob Horner, Doug Guess, Bob and Lynn Koegel, Pat Mirenda, and many others listed with a series of titles credited to each of them. The research and program design of this group helps us to understand the messages of others and to teach the skills they need most.

Originally, this body of research asked us to listen to the actions of individuals who failed to use words and to accept those actions as their most powerful form of communication. To stop with only those who had significant communication difficulties or significant intellectual challenges would have made communicative intent a path for only a few, rather than most. Given the volume of today's literature base, we know much more than we did some twenty years ago. We now know that communicative intent is not an issue of disability at all. Not using words is commonplace for most individuals in our society. In other words, using actions to transmit messages between individuals is a fact of life.

Caller ID is a high-tech form of using non-verbal means to allow us to screen our phone calls. The need for Caller ID would be greatly reduced if we, as individuals, would simply let unwelcome callers know we do not welcome their call. We could make our declaration either before a person attempted the call or in the initial seconds of the call. But we prefer using technology to do our work. So, we must accept the notion that the actions of most individuals convey communicative messages. And these non-verbal messages are a preferred way of communication by most individuals, including most individuals with disabilities.

Taking the above perspective on communication, what is the path for using communicative intent to better map out behavior and a means to change? The path starts with identifying the individual's behavior that is causing such turmoil for the person as well as the others around him or her.

- Identify the behavioral challenge.
- Assume the behavior is communicative and work under that assumption.
- Hypothesize (lacking any science) what possible messages could be relayed through this behavior(s).
- Assume that using behavior to relay a message means the individual lacks other ways to express the same message.
- Identify what skills the individual might need to learn to express needs more clearly, gently, and carefully.
- Design ways to address the teaching of those skills within the classroom, workplace, and home.

It is imperative that we understand that this is a teaching model. Why? This model operates daily on behalf of students in every classroom in this country, as well as for many of us at work. Listening to a person's actions is a strategy used by every one of us, in the following ways:

◆

An individual comes to work appearing tired and withdrawn. She just isn't herself. She is meek and is not engaged in the bustle of the workplace.

We start to wonder if she ate breakfast before coming to work. We wonder if her frail grandmother died over the weekend. We ask ourselves if her family might have been evicted again from their house and are now living in their car. We wonder about the state of her parents' marriage – maybe the split finally happened.

◆

A student mispronounces over half of the words in a story. The student seems to be confused regarding the vowel sounds, long and short. He is pretty confident when it comes to consonants, but his overall fluency is greatly impacted by his inability to read without making errors.

We start asking ourselves if he might not hear the vowels sounds clearly. We wonder what type of reading program he had in his previous class or school. We wonder if he has ever been exposed to a direct instruction reading curriculum. We wonder if he has an auditory processing challenge that has gone undetected until now.

◆

Although these examples are fictitious, they are prime examples of the kinds of responses we have to the people we know. Reading into the intent of another's actions is commonplace. It is one way we show people we care and desire to understand them as best we can.

Asking ourselves to make this commitment to the people we serve, teach, employ, and support is just an extension of this practice. So if we believe in the process of listening to the actions of people in academic, vocational, and social/emotional venues, why aren't human service and educational professionals using it to view behavior in general?

I think the answer is quite simple. We are caught up in the mythology of behavior management and behavior modification. We relish the idea of using a "science" to address issues brought to us by students and our co-workers.

Also, by holding onto the mythology of the behavioral sciences, we can maintain our beliefs that individuals are solely responsible for their actions and challenges. We want to view them as:

- people in complete control of their actions
- people rationally choosing which behavior they might use
- people always acting intentionally and deliberately
- people fitting all the labels we are so comfortable applying to them.

We are far too likely to lay blame and responsibility on someone who talks out in class, who steals from others, who hits or kicks others, or who wipes their bodily materials onto our bodies. These are the individuals who might benefit from communicative intent even more than others.

So is it as simple as that? Is it simply including the most disruptive and destructive individuals into a process that we already use everyday? I believe the answer is, without a doubt, "Yes!"

Generating Lists of Possibilities: Communicative Intent

Let's look where the process of understanding behavior might take us if we were determined to make it work. Let's take the example of stealing, a common enough behavior and one that has significant impact on an individual, its victims, and a setting. If we believed that the person was trying to tell us something through the act of stealing from others, what might those possible communications be?

STEALING

I want it.
I need it.
I know stealing – it is I – I am it.
I live in a culture of stealing.
I want to impact another person.
I never get caught.
Others steal; why not me?
My friends steal.
Stealing gains me friends/status.
Stealing/being problematic is my identity.
I just borrowed it – you call it stealing.
Someone said I could have it.
Stealing creates my sense of worth.
Stealing makes my life OK.
I like taking risks.
I simply defy authority – stealing is only one way.
I have been stealing for years – no big deal.
I didn't know it was wrong.
I don't think it hurts anyone.
Someone gave it to me.
Things have been stolen from me.
I need to stay out of trouble with ___.
I did it on a dare.
I need things to trade.

Let's look at a few more behavioral examples before we examine what we have and where we go.

SPEAKING OUT INAPPROPRIATELY

I have an idea/I must tell someone.
I didn't know it's not OK.
I don't get asked to speak.
If I don't talk out, I don't get to tell others.
I am unaware of the system.
I have no storage system/I refuse to lose my ideas.
My ideas are very important to me.
Talking is my strength, my identity.
Writing and reading are my weaknesses.
I want to be known for my strengths.
Others talk out.
I can't predict being called on.
I need to be in control.
I want to disrupt.
I can't catch myself before I act on my ideas.
I know how to "bug" the teacher or the boss.
I want others to respect/like me.
I want others to lose.
I want peer contact/attention.
I am simply defiant.
I don't like the rules.
I did not make the rules.
Following rules works only for certain people.
I want recognition for what I know.
It's my way of maintaining my self-esteem.

Although some behaviors are more destructive and maybe more common-place, we can apply the process to more unusual actions or the lack of those actions. Seeing the variations in human behavior brings a better understanding of how powerful an inclusive process might be for the individual and for ourselves as we strive to provide the right kind of support.

FAILING TO VOLUNTEER

I'm shy.
I have poor self-esteem.
I don't know information required.
I'm angry.
I'm insecure.
I'm lazy.
My culture doesn't volunteer.
I can't take a risk.
I've got nothing to gain.
I don't want to go against the social norm.
I get publicly anxious.
I'm bored.
I feel inadequate/incompetent.
I have low self-esteem.
I don't know the answers.
I have low cognitive skills.
I have low language skills.

And of course, some behaviors are what bring results for many children. Their attempts to communicate are attended to by others without any hesitation. Crying is one of the human actions that falls into that category. We are immediately drawn in by someone's crying as we look for the possible reasons someone would be in such distress. Crying offers many traditional possibilities, but also provides us new ways of seeing an old thing.

CRYING

I am unhappy/hurt emotionally.
I have physical pain/problems.
I want attention.
I don't know what to do.
I am frustrated.
I have fears.
I feel angry.
I want to avoid work.
I want self-indulgence.
I want power/control.
I feel stress.
I lack verbal/social skills to express feelings.
I'm afraid.
I'm emotionally overloaded.
I have emotional problems.
I have poor self-esteem.
I feel inadequate and incompetent.
I have raging hormones.
I'm acting my developmental age.
I'm overwhelmed.
I'm hungry.

Instead of labeling the person as criminal, spoiled, attention-seeking, or disruptive, move comfortably into the "world of possibilities" with me. These lists tell a story of many differently complicated individuals or of a single highly complex person. That is the important distinction brought about by this process. We are not looking for the magic pill. On the contrary, we are hoping to make sense of a meaningful sequence of events in another's life.

We are moving in this direction as we abandon previous practices. Hopefully, we will let go of labeling individuals for the sake of making them appear aberrant. Creating lists of possible communications will assist us in leaving behind the mythology of behavior management. Provided with a new process, we can now pull away from a mythology that does not allow for creativity and vision, but simply asks us to view the person as a flawed variable in a scientific equation.

At this point we are wearing the new glasses as we avoid the quicksand of behavior modification. We are following a new direction with a new purpose to our investigation. We are armed, not with data and labels, but with possibilities and vision. We are now looking at the non-verbal messages a person might be sending us that speak to his or her humanity, needs, vulnerabilities, and lack of wholeness. We are on the threshold of seeing a person from a whole new perspective.

Guidelines that Govern the Creation of Possibility Lists

To move to selecting the one or more possibilities that might fit a person and his or her behaviors, one must know the individual well enough to see the situation through his or her eyes. Highly trained professionals who rarely visit and know little about the individual can be a part of our team, but they must understand the limitations of their role as a decision maker.

The list should include all ideas and possibilities. It is important to recognize that these lists represent a "brainstorming" effort undertaken by the people who know the individual well. As in all brainstorming activities, all suggestions are listed without critique from others.

As I look back at the lists in the Appendix (page 83), which I have developed over many years, I see some pretty crazy ideas, But they have all proven valuable at times, so I have preserved them. I vividly recall a teacher from Ft. Bragg, California, listing "I am teaching my shoes to walk," as a possible communicative intent for "out of seat behavior." Now that is creative! And it came only from opening one's mind to the possibilities of what an individual might be saying through his or her actions.

As soon as we start critiquing and limiting the possibilities, the lists will shrink and we will probably start to see the reproduction of the "labeling" that placed limitations on our thinking. I say this because I have worked with teams of people who could not make the leap into a new thinking. They could only create lists that labeled the individual as aggressive, hurtful, or mean. That is the last thing we would ever want at this point in the process.

So what do we do with these lists? Once again, we need to remember that only the closest players have the most valid information at this point in the process. One might now ask, "How about the individual joining in at this point?" If you are thinking that, I am cheering you on!

Many professionals have told me that once they have brought in the individual, he or she was able to help pinpoint his or her communicative intent. The lists provide possibilities that paint the individual in incredibly positive ways. Move over and let them in!

For now the task is pretty clear. As a team of individuals who know and care about the person, we need to make some choices from the list. We need to test the ones that make real sense to us and to the individual.

CHAPTER FOUR

◆◆◆

Teaching for Change,
Change for Teaching

Here is one of the most powerful stories I have ever seen unfold. I was doing training for a county school system in the Bay Area of California about ten years ago. A wonderful mix of teachers represented many differently labeled students within their system. One teacher, Roberta, taught a self-contained classroom for high school students with learning disabilities.

Pamela, a student in Roberta's classroom, heroically played the role of "class clown," demanding and getting everyone's attention whenever she chose. Pamela was a major disruption to Roberta's efforts to teach the class.

As we did our brainstorming and thinking about Pamela's communicative intent, we struggled to stay clear of all the negative labels and stereotypical ways of looking at these behaviors in a classroom. Pamela posed a very difficult puzzle for the group as we tried to create our possibility list. But, we prevailed. From that list, we decided to start with the following:

Pamela wanted someone to care about her, really care about her,
through thick and thin, good and bad, hell or high water –
someone who liked her for who she was, not who she could be.

From that starting point, Roberta returned from our latest training session determined to find a way to tell Pamela how much she cared about her. Before leaving the session, we discussed how Roberta might approach teaching Pamela that she was cared about.

We talked about Roberta telling her things openly and how Pamela might simply throw them back in her face. We talked about giving her written messages and what Pamela might do with those. Finally, Roberta decided to try both written and verbal messages to see how Pamela responded.

Knowing she could not say anything too personal in the beginning, Roberta remarked about Pamela's new shoes as she entered the classroom. Immediately, Pamela drew everyone's attention to her teacher's comment.

Roberta confirmed what we had all feared. Pamela could not let the messages be received in front of the class without some form of "look what the teacher said about me." Pamela took her traditional stance and made fun of the comment regardless of its complimentary nature. Pamela was not going to be taken in by a teacher who liked her shoes, no way!

Roberta was crushed. She wanted to let Pamela know how much she cared about her for who she was, but continually ran into Pamela's "in your face" responses.

Although Roberta continued to try to reach out to Pamela in small ways, she felt pretty hopeless for the next two weeks. She was hesitant to venture too far into this quicksand again until she was better prepared to deliver her message in a safer way.

As Roberta waited not knowing what to do, Pamela solved the problem. It came about two weeks after the initial fiasco. Pamela walked into the classroom with a new haircut. She turned to Roberta and asked, "What do you think of my hair?"

Whether or not Roberta had felt a complete failure in her efforts to befriend Pamela, she had started a process of building a unique relationship with Pamela. Whether Roberta had chosen the right place to start or the right comment to make, Pamela had heard her despite the fact that she had also thrown it all back in Roberta's face.

With that question looming in front of her, Roberta felt the immediate connection to what Pamela was asking. Roberta knew then that she had been right and that beneath all of Pamela's pretending and acting, there was a vulnerable young woman seeking the approval of her teacher.

Of course, Roberta leaped on the chance to compliment Pamela on her haircut. For to have failed at that moment would have taught Pamela the wrong thing – that Roberta really did not care about her, but was merely out to find a weak spot in Pamela's armor, a place to use against her at a later time.

And so the story started to change for Roberta and Pamela. Every time Roberta attended training, we were eager to hear how things had been going for the two women. At our last training session, Roberta told about Pamela spending more time working on schoolwork and less time being disruptive.

Pamela grew closer and closer to Roberta as time passed. Roberta told us how Pamela approached her to tell her that she did not want to leave early for lunch that day. Roberta really felt pleased about this, because despite their relationship developing in the classroom, lunchtime still spelled "trouble" for Pamela. Lunch was the time when she would do her most risky activities, which generally involved sex and drugs.

Roberta was quick to tell Pamela she did not have to leave for lunch. Pamela sealed the occasion by telling Roberta, "I really don't want to go out to lunch, today. Could I stay in and have lunch with you?"

Who would have thought that Pamela would give up being the "class clown" and turn away from friends and a risky lifestyle for the relationship one teacher was willing to undertake. But it happened and it continued to happen for those two young women.

Roberta's willingness to see Pamela differently and to approach her and her issues in a new way created a fertile place for Pamela's change to happen. It took no magic, no mythology, no behavioral data, no ABC charts. It took only one teacher to take a risk in developing a relationship, with the hope that her student might join her in that risk.

Having been part of that story so many years ago still feels like a privilege to me. It is stories like Roberta and Pamela's that have kept my beliefs alive.

So what do we do with those possibility lists we are going to make for challenging individuals? Let's go back to Ellen from the first chapter. Ellen was doing things that drove people away from her. She ended up being blamed for acts that were seen as unclean and disgusting. Her teachers were able to see only the negative attributes of her actions. They were unable to see her actions as communicative and highly expressive.

Without a process that focuses on communicative intent of another's actions, this group of professionals could not positively support Ellen. If they saw her "sliming" as a game she played with others, they could identify a place to start.

What we believe:

Playing games with friends is normal and personal. Ellen was very successful at playing games. Games tend to be most beneficial to both people if they are reciprocal and mutual.

Ellen's view of playing games lacks both of these important features. So if we label what might be wrong with Ellen's game playing, we would have to say, "It lacked turn-taking, reciprocity, and mutuality."

Those are the areas of development to target as we teach Ellen more about playing with others. It is not all Ellen's fault that she lacked these understandings. Through the actions of many educators, Ellen had been taught an incorrect assumption about how humans interact through games.

For many years, no one was able to accept Ellen's playfulness as genuine and sincere. They had always seen it as aberrant and in need of behavior modification. So for many years, Ellen learned the only thing she could successfully pull off – play your part of the game before anyone could scold you for your actions. If you wait for them to teach you how to play, they will only try to stop your playing entirely.

What we need to teach and how we might approach that teaching:

In this case, we would go into Ellen's situation with new interactive games to teach reciprocity and mutuality. We would probably want to go with Ellen's lead and take her interactions as our starting point.

With the "nose touching" game, it was possible to engage Ellen in something she liked to do, to provide an experience in which both persons had a role to play, and, finally, to teach Ellen that reciprocal games have a longer life span. It was the same scenario with the "hitting" game. We made it a game where both persons had roles and both persons played out those roles through "turn taking."

It must be added that Ellen is not going to create these options on her own. Without a healthy understanding of what makes a good interactive game, Ellen is not going to understand what is lacking in the game. She is not going to seek out her own solution.

If we use behavior modification to stop the "sliming," we could eliminate Ellen's limited means of being playful without providing her any further outlet(s) for her playfulness. But when we ask sincerely playful people to stop playing because we don't like their games, we are fundamentally asking them to become different people to better suit our likes and dislikes.

It is only through providing possible alternatives to the "gotcha scheme" that we begin to create a path for learning and change. Any change that creates a place for Ellen to retain her art of self-expression – playfulness – starts with the teaching of mutually beneficial games.

That teaching is our responsibility. Ellen's responsibility to change only follows our lead. This was true for Ellen, a person with significant intellectual challenges, as well as it was for Pamela. It is our lead that creates the path. Without that healthy lead, their change is not to be anticipated nor expected.

Now, let's return to Dennis, the fifth-year high school student who would not wear his shoes. Let's not undervalue his need to wear his shoes. But we must consider Dennis' perspective and ask the right questions to help us support both his needs and his behavioral challenges in a better way. Simply holding to a behavior plan that has proven ineffective and limiting Dennis' education is not adequate nor supportive of Dennis and his challenges.

We need to approach his challenges in a different way – the communicative intent way. We want to investigate if there is another way of seeing his actions so that we could provide the teaching required to match his personal needs. From that focus, a list of possible communicative intents might look like the following:

I don't like wearing shoes.

I don't need my shoes; I am not going anywhere.

I am mad about something.

My shoes hurt my feet.

I don't want to go anywhere.

I know it makes you mad.

I can't trust that we are really going anywhere.

Keeping my shoes on does not enhance my school day.

It's the only way I have to say what I need to say. It means lots of things.

You don't listen to me if I do everything as expected.

I get lots of attention.

I am just saying, "No!"

I don't know what I should anticipate happening.

Sometimes I get to do great things; sometimes I just sit.

Most of the time, you don't care if I have my shoes on.

What we believe:

From my years of knowing Dennis, I always worked on the assumption that he did not believe anything good would come from wearing his shoes. I also believed that he was telling me that removing his shoes was his mildest way of protesting what was happening.

What we need to teach and how we might approach that teaching:

It was the goal to teach Dennis that, together, we were going to have very productive days at high school. From too many years of idle time during his reduced school day, Dennis had been taught that there was absolutely no reason to come prepared to do anything. Getting his expectations up for a productive school experience had only left him disappointed.

From the instruction of many, Dennis had learned that it was no one's job to create experiences for him. Therefore, why wear shoes? This explanation for Dennis' challenges with his footwear makes total sense when you consider his actions as messages telling us clearly what he had learned from his teachers.

It was also true that Dennis had very limited means of expressing himself. Removing his shoes had become his generic protest. As a matter of fact, recently while Dennis was staying at our house, we were preparing to help some friends give him a haircut. Now, Dennis dislikes having his haircut and it is not an easy feat. I am sure that many parents can relate to this story, because many children resist haircuts, tooth brushing, and all those highly intrusive experiences that are necessary in life. We decided to wet Dennis' hair in anticipation of the friends arriving and the beginning of the haircut. After we sprayed his hair, his shoes slipped off. He was just saying, "I don't like that and I am not looking forward to this haircut!"

So facing the challenge of demonstrating to Dennis, on a daily basis, that we are going to have experiences in which he will excel, meet people, and enjoy being outside, we set up a schedule that included all those components. In the beginning, Dennis challenged my sincerity almost daily by removing his shoes.

Over time, Dennis came to expect our routine and taking off his shoes simply faded away. As the shoes became less and less of an issue at school, Dennis was wearing them more and more for his mother when they were out doing chores in town. Actually, his need to question wearing shoes was really brilliant on his part. Could his questioning the need for shoes have been the most important question anyone was bothering to ask?

That question needed a clear and concrete answer from all of us through our actions. I use the term "actions" as our responsibility simply because words were not as powerful to Dennis as were actions. The idea of stating in words, "Dennis, you need to have your shoes on because it is time to go to PE class," was no way of answering his question about the need for him to keep his shoes on. He needed to be in PE class daily so that he could start to trust his need for shoes.

Fundamentally, the order of these events helps define the difference between communicative intent and behavioral manipulation. It is far too common to dangle the event requiring the shoes in front of an individual as a reward for behavior compliance. Instead, we should provide the event so that an individual will learn why shoes are important to the enrichment of their lives.

By proving the need for shoes as a teaching process, we offer Dennis a chance. Maybe later, much later, he would hear your words and respond by not removing the shoes. But in the beginning, he needed to see it all happening on a regular basis. Once again, Dennis changed in response to our changes. We changed his need for shoes by creating real experiences for him.

After he started to believe and trust in us, his shoes just stayed on. His need to tell me that nothing important was going to happen in school was not pressing. I did not ask him to stop telling me about what others had failed to do. I just chose to take his non-verbal message as my challenge:

> *I don't like wearing shoes...I don't need my shoes, I am not going*
> *anywhere... I am mad about something...My shoes hurt my feet...*
> *I don't want to go anywhere...I know it makes you mad... I can't*
> *trust that we are really going anywhere...Keeping my shoes on*
> *does not enhance my school day...It's the only way I have to say*
> *what I need to say. It means lots of things...You don't listen to me*
> *if I do everything as expected....I get lots of attention...I am just*
> *saying, "No!"...I don't know what I should anticipate happening...*
> *Sometimes I get to do great things; sometimes I just sit...*
> *Most of the time, you don't care if I have my shoes on...*

Now, let's try an example from our "stealing" list.

STEALING
I want it.
I need it.
I know stealing – it is I – I am it.
I live in a culture of stealing.
I want to impact another person.
I never get caught.

Others steal/why not me?
My friends steal.
Stealing gains me friends/status.
Stealing/being problematic is my identity.
I just borrowed it – you call it stealing.
Someone said I could have it.
Stealing creates my sense of worth.
Stealing makes my life OK.
I like taking risks.
I simply defy authority.
I have been stealing for years – no big deal.
I didn't know it was wrong.
I don't think it hurts anyone.
Someone gave it to me.
Things are stolen from me.
I need to stay out of trouble with ___.
I did it on a dare.
I need things to trade.

Many individuals have challenged those who support or teach them by stealing. Children pick up things off their teachers' desk while they are busy with another student. A worker steals from his or her employer. A person steals from a store.

Many times, the teacher or staff will question whether or not the individual actually understands the impact "stealing" has on another individual. They might question whether or not the person felt anything for the victim of his or her actions. This always poses an interesting entry point for dealing with the challenge of stealing from a communicative perspective. So let's look at the possibilities of believing the person is saying, *"I don't think it hurts anyone..."*

What we believe:

What we might learn about the individual is that he or she truly does not understand how personally a victim is impacted by a thief. I recall the one and only time I had an automobile stolen from in front of my house. It was like someone had violated me. I did not have any distance from the rawness of the crime. I felt a deep resentment of those individuals and was hurt by their actions. I could not let go of the impact I felt. Most individuals who have experienced theft would be quick to label the feelings they felt when they became aware of their loss.

In this case, we must assume the student does not understand or prioritize the impact of being the victim of a theft. As a skill or learned understanding, we must assume the individual first of all lacks the experience or knowledge of being a victim.

What we need to teach and how we might approach that teaching:

When we teach empathy, we have to be clear that stealing is a personal act that happens between people. It might be that the thief can maintain a "distanced" view of the act, but that is not the same for the victim. Without the human connection as the focus of our teaching, we will always fail to connect the actions of the thief to the humanity of the victim.

How do we help the person have empathy for a potential victim? Some ideas might be:
1. Carefully role-play the theft of a dearly-held object and discuss feelings.
2. Teach the needed understandings through literature.
3. Have a group discussion about the topic in which others relate stories of their experiences as a victim.
4. Help the individual comprehend the impact of stealing by discussing a situation where the person can feel the victim role. That could be any area where he or she does not excel or feel vulnerable. By building on this life experience, we can help the person go into the world of someone from whom he or she is stealing.

These possible teaching foci are aimed at providing the individual an experience to learn about being a victim. What we choose for the teaching will be individualized for the specific person. It needs to be taught with the understanding that your relationship will endure the "pain" the person might experience.

In this case, we are endeavoring to teach an emotional response and not an academic skill. For this reason, you should be careful how you select a strategy and be ready to support the person in his or her learning. In many ways, this example gets to the core of being human and must be done with great finesse. This example is more risky than most and should be seen as a very intense teaching/learning experience.

On the other hand, what if we started with another possible answer, such as *"I need to stay out of trouble with [one who values stealing], and the best way to do this is by demonstrating stealing"* then we would need to see our methods and objectives very differently. So what might we do in this situation?

What we believe:

There is a relationship that exists between the individual and another person that is perpetuating this dynamic. The individual is either using poor judgment in the selection of "significant others" or feels trapped in a relationship with another person. From here, we would start to construct possible learning scenarios and strategies that to help the person to move away from the "entrapment."

What we need to teach and how we might approach that teaching:

First, we could introduce the individual to others who are not involved in "proving themselves." Through their model, maybe the individual could see a way out of the situation.

We could arrange for the individual to work with those who need help in one of his or her "strength" areas. This arrangement might create a new dynamic based on the same "I need approval from another person or group" scenario. In this case, the expectations for the individual might replace a peer's detrimental expectations.

We could take a huge leap and arrange for the individual to become a leader in a project that requires the handling of valuable items or money. We might help arrange a job where he or she would be expected to choose honesty over loyalty. For example, we could have a fundraising project and assign the person the role of treasurer. In this case, the expectations of the group might override the expectations of a single individual.

We could simply entrust the individual with a piece of valuable information or possession of our own. We would use the language of "trustworthy" rather than "thief" or "dependency."

These examples of supporting the challenges of someone who steals from others opens new doors for re-thinking positive support and clearly positions "teaching" as the direction of our efforts.

Let's turn our attention to our "speaks out at inappropriate times" list. Some of these communications might include students in the classroom or adults with disabilities who interrupt or talk inappropriately in other environments, such as at work. First, let's review the list again.

SPEAKING OUT INAPPROPRIATELY

I have an idea/I must tell someone.
I didn't know it's not OK.
I don't get asked to speak.
If I don't talk out, I don't get to tell others.
I am unaware of the system.
I have no storage system/I refuse to lose my ideas.
My ideas are very important to me.
Talking is my strength, my identity.
Writing and reading are my weaknesses.
I want to be known for my strengths.
Others talk out.
I can't predict being called on.
I need to be in control.
I want to disrupt.
I can't catch myself before I act on my ideas.
I know how to "bug" the teacher or the boss.
I want others to respect/like me.
I want others to lose.
I want peer contact/attention.
I am simply defiant.
I don't like the rules.
I did not make the rules.
Following rules only works for certain people.
I want recognition for what I know.
It's my way of maintaining my self-esteem.

I have highlighted six possibilities in bold because I have come to believe that many of the issues embedded in these six are common issues for children and adults with disabilities. I would like to take them on individually so that you might better understand what messages those we serve might have.

1) I don't get asked to speak.

What we believe:

If people are giving us this message, they are telling us about favoritism and prejudice from the adults in their life. If a person really feels ignored by key people in his or her life, it paints a depressing picture. What is likely running through this person's mind is a feeling of worthlessness and invisibility.

What we need to teach and how we might approach that teaching:

Our initial response to this message requires our acknowledgement of individuals as valuable people within the setting. If we can't do this by asking them to share their ideas, we must find a way for them to excel in some venue.

If we are really going to address the intent of the message, we need to examine our relationship with each person. This type of message is difficult to hear and it will also be difficult to answer.

I cannot count the number of students who have sat quietly in their seats and were not receiving even the basic acknowledgement from the adults within the school. This happens because quiet students rank below noisy ones in drawing our attention. The same is true of many adults with disabilities. It is a sad reality. Making a quiet person feel valued is not an easy task, because we are so focused on the disruptive and attention-seeking ones. Nonetheless, if the message is sincere, we need to find a way to include that person.

2) I have no storage system/I refuse to lose my ideas.

What we believe:

In this case, we are allowing ourselves to see the person as someone who lacks either a place to store ideas in the brain or who cannot retrieve the information after successfully storing it. Of course, these two notions lead us to consider a processing problem that might exist in either of these forms.

What we need to teach and how we might approach that teaching:

After looking at all the possibilities, one fourth-grade teacher felt this message had a reasonable fit for a student in her class. Most remarkably, the teacher agreed she would provide the student with a tape recorder for capturing his ideas without feeling the need to blurt them out to the entire class. The teacher also agreed she would listen to the tape daily as she drove home from school. She would then be ready to respond to some of the ideas the following day.

If successful, the student would learn that his ideas were not destined to be lost if he did not call out during class. I have always cherished the motivation of the teacher to try something this radical for a typical fourth grader. I also have cherished being able to tell audiences over many years that it did not work.

The student did not provide a tape full of comments for the teacher although he did stop talking out in class. While we were willing to take a lead from a single possibility on the list, it just was not the correct one. So why did the talking out stop? Maybe we should have looked at it from this possibility to better understand why change happened. Maybe we should have started off with the following possible communicative intent:

3) I can't catch myself before I act on my ideas.

What we believe:

Not unlike many, this person spoke out before he realized it might not be the right thing to do. In this case, we might be dealing more specifically with learning modality rather that a processing problem.

For this individual, hearing a reactive response from the person in charge did not help prevent a reoccurrence of talking out. Being able to look down at a tape recorder at his workspace made the real difference. That visual reminder helped him remember to think about blurting out an answer.

What we need to teach and how we might approach that teaching:

The shift from a reactive verbal response to a proactive visual reminder made the change possible for this individual. So, we chose the wrong possibility in the beginning, but our mistake helped us learn more about the person.

Sometimes, we simply will stumble into the answer and that is OK. It is OK to err when choosing from the lists because what we will try typically will not harm the individual. In this case, it was not hurtful, degrading, or punishing for this person to have a tape recorder on his workspace.

On the contrary, the person might have felt honored that someone was going out on a limb in an attempt to help. Our mistake brought us back to the list to see what we had failed to recognize in our first attempt. The tape recorder could stay with the person or we could find another visual reminder better suited for a fourth grader.

I vividly remember the teacher's frustration and her personal commitment to this student. It was my suggestion that got that tape recorder on the student's desk, but it was her relationship with her student that made it happen. And when we realized we had not chosen the right possible communicative intent, her relationship with her student brought out the true nature of his challenge.

4) Talking is my strength, my identity.

What we believe:

What we learn from accepting this communication is a very humbling message. Like all of us, Juanita wanted to be seen as gifted in an area. Her skill as a "talker" felt better than her other skills.

To feel good about her capacities, she chose to talk as much as she could despite the disruption it might bring. So what did she fail to recognize in herself? It is hard to believe that any of us have a sole strength. So maybe she failed to see herself as talented in other areas. Maybe she was a good athlete, but did not equate that as important. Maybe she had other gifts, but they were overshadowed by her overall struggle to learn.

In writing about this situation, I cannot help but think about the story of Roberta and Pamela that opened this chapter. Roberta's single approach to seeing herself as the class clown is not all that different from the student who invests totally in her ability to talk as her sole identity. By helping her see herself as a broader person, her teacher Pamela was able to make the beginning steps in supporting her.

What we need to teach and how we might approach that teaching:

If our hypothesis is correct, it is our job to help Juanita identify her array of strengths and talents so that she can see herself as a well-rounded individual. This is an issue that might plague many students and adults with disabilities, especially those in special education classrooms and human service programs.

For individuals who struggle to learn, it must be challenging to see themselves as talented and gifted. If you do find a activity where you shine, you would want to do that activity as much as possible. I jokingly tell audiences that I'd rather they know me as a presenter than as a basketball player. I, too, know my strengths. We all do.

5) I can't predict being called on.

What we believe:

Once again, this is a fundamental message that gets to the core of how we relate to our world. An educator will strive to create clear paths so that students can see what's coming and can make sense of their routines. On the other hand, for those students who do not see the patterns, school life and learning is random and challenging.

Predictability creates trust between individuals as well as between an individual and a system. As humans, we strive to find trusting relationships with people and things. In order to achieve that goal, we create our own trust – we will provide our own patterns. In these extreme moments, it is understandable that students might find themselves at odds with a classroom management system.

It is perfectly possible that an individual would talk out to create predictable patterns to his or her day. Even though the patterns one might create would be negative feedback, it is, most importantly, predictable feedback. We are oftentimes puzzled why someone would bring so much negative focus to themselves. But we must remember that when someone is striving for predictable feedback, feedback is feedback regardless of whether it is positive or negative.

What we need to teach and how we might approach that teaching:

Educator or human service professionals are responsible for creating order and predictability for those they support and teach. In many cases, those we teach come from homes where predictability is lacking. When they arrive at school or an adult services program, they need to see how the system will provide routines, schedules, activities, progress, assistance, and enjoyment in a patterned and predictable way.

For the individual who feels cheated by our system in this arena, we need to make the utmost effort to ensure that the person sees the routines, schedules, activities, progress, assistance, and enjoyment in a manner that creates a trust for them. We might have to provide a visual schedule, a start-finish pattern to work assignments, a list of individuals being called on, or a day planner for that individual. We will be responsible for making sure that the person sees the patterns that we feel are quite obvious.

6) I am simply defiant.

What we believe:

Over the years, I have heard many individuals described as defiant. I know that a percentage of those are truly acting defiantly. What has often bothered me is the triviality of their defiance. Believing that a person's actions are saying, "I know the rules and simply refuse to follow them," leaves us looking for an outlet for the defiance. Could it be that we will need to find another place for their defiance to be meaningful and purposeful while not being disruptive and challenging?

What we need to teach and how we might approach that teaching:

As someone who has been defiant in my lifetime, I understand its value to our society. I would assume that we all see value in acts of defiance. But to act out one's defiance in a classroom, home, or work setting, simply for the sake of not following expectations, seems of little value to our society, to peers, or to those who teach and support.

I would hope that our teaching focus would be to enlighten the person to the value of defiant acts targeted in specific ways. No setting is without a need for change. Let people seek real change through their defiance, not through talking out in class. Let an agency change because workers express their defiance in group meetings and as members of the governing boards of the nonprofit organization.

Similarly, every community needs social activists. There are real causes that require real solutions. I have always asked professionals to focus someone's defiance in a real direction. Help save endangered species, create recycling programs at the school or workplace, feed and assist people who are homeless, stop domestic violence – these are real causes that can require real defiance on an individual's part. Let's ask "defiant" people to use their energy in a venue that will not change without their focus.

In closing this chapter, I hope you have seen the many directions the possibility lists might take us. That is why creating each list is so very important! The more diverse the list, the greater array of possibilities to try. The greater the array of possibilities, the more varied our teaching approaches will be as we teach for change.

CHAPTER FIVE
◆◆◆

Unforgivable Omissions, Knowing Better

After thinking about how we might read behavior in our attempts to better support people, there are specific issues that relate to communicative intent and what we eventually decide to do for and against people with behavioral challenges. The notion that behavior support is a simple undertaking is erroneous. The field of behavioral understanding has opened up door after door, thanks to many good scholars who have devoted their careers to expanding the possibilities for supportive behavior work. We must consider all the possibilities if we are going to feel proud of what we understand.

First Do No Harm

This is part of the physician's Hippocratic Oath as a provider of health care. We need to have the same commitment to the people we serve. Needless to say, a great deal of injury and bad feelings has accompanied behavior modification. We tend to place responsibility for change on the individual without acknowledging the cost that individual might pay for being pressured into making changes.

Let's look back at Ellen from Chapter One, who has paid dearly for her inability to please others. I recall her coming to high school with the mythology that she liked to watch jazzercise video tapes. Years before, when I observed her, on behalf of her parents, I could see that the tapes were being used for more than just rewards.

What I saw was teachers putting Ellen in front of the TV/video and leaving her on her own. In addition, they responded to any deviation into negative behavior by removing Ellen from the TV/video or denying her the right to view the tape. Ellen's initial indication of her preference had been carried to an extreme without anyone asking if it was fair to turn her preference into a reward and, more commonly, a punishment.

I never actually had put much faith in the video tapes and I immediately felt it was a devious and unhealthy thing to use with Ellen. I must admit that I gave the videos a try in high school and they did not work. Ellen is a very social person and the video did not replace the human contact and attention she truly enjoyed. So, she would leave the TV/video in search of someone with whom to interact.

It was clear, Ellen had no desire to be left with the video. Its value to her was far less important than others would have professed. So where did all these beliefs about Ellen and jazzercise tapes come from? Did anyone really believe the mythology? What had truly come from Ellen's early interest in the tapes? If our intent is to manipulate individuals into doing what we ask, then when we discover a preference or distaste for a particular activity, we use the activity as a tool for manipulation.

So how does that cause harm and damage to the individual? It takes only a short time for people to understand that they had better not show preferences and dislikes, because it will be used against them tomorrow and in the future.

That understanding turns into distrust and fear of others. And it should! When did we start believing that it is our right to teach others to distrust us? Isn't our role to teach that we will honor those with whom we work and listen carefully to what they tell us? Isn't it a partnership where we walk together promising not to do things that will cause harm and hurt?

In the process we have learned in this text, we can work with individuals for change without inflicting harm. This is because we precede the individual into the change. We take careful steps in our change process that make their following us safer.

Let's go back to the fourth grade boy who was guilty of talking out in class. By hypothesizing the communicative intent of his behavior, we chose something related to his not being able to store and retrieve information. As a result of the hypothesis, his instructor gave him a tape recorder to store his ideas on a cassette tape. It was the instructor's intent to listen to the tape after school or on the drive home so she could try to respond to some of his ideas the following day.

Quickly it became known that our hypothesis was not correct and we needed to think differently about the talking out problem. Immediately, we should ask ourselves if we have damaged this young boy in any way. Because we made decisions based on communicative intent, we can feel confident that we did not inflict harm or pain. Our decision might have caused us to try unnecessary, redundant, and over-simplified interventions, but nothing was hurtful. And best of all, we might have learned some very important information through our errors that, when they are corrected, will make change more accessible to the individual.

We may have made a mistake and asked the individual to do something that was not particularly helpful, but we did not cause the boy to feel bad about himself. That is the difference between simplistic behavior modification and analyzing communicative intent. And that difference aids us in our commitment to the Hippocratic Oath.

Relationships

I have discussed how important your relationship with the individual is if you are going to ask for change. In a training last year, I was appalled that adults were asking others, whose names they did not know, to change. Change is a very delicate and risky process for anyone. Being connected to an individual is the only ticket that allows us to ask for change. It is your initiating your own change in viewing their behavior that solidifies the relationship.

As we have discussed, most situations using this process ask a great deal more of an instructor than simply teaching academics or job tasks. The closeness of the adult and the individual makes their relationship even more critical. And in many cases, your relationship may be the only one that has been offered to the individual in an honest and sincere way.

Being a "willing-to-take-a-chance" adult separates you from the dozens of others who predated your involvement with an individual. I have never understood how to teach without first establishing a relationship based on truth and predictability. It is the granite of a good educator. It is not the dessert of teaching; it is the main course.

Many individuals need to learn about trust before they are ready to learn about information and skills. Learning to mistrust people and systems comes naturally. It is often the outcome of bad teaching and the overuse of behavior modification.

It is usually noticeable to an observer whether an individual has been taught through ineffective or bad teaching before any relationships have been established. In any setting, you will find people who stand up to tell others they want attention. Why is this? Because when they are not standing up, no one comes over to talk to them – it is that simple. If you want someone to talk to you, you cannot be sitting down. Why? Because many teaching relationships have set that pattern with the learner and everyone learns how to make the best of a situation. So, standing up becomes the rule but then likely will be identified as a problem needing an intervention.

I would go as far as to challenge people to examine their relationships with the individuals they serve. Note, however, that you can not or should not expect yourself to establish strong relationships with every individual you serve. That is simply impossible. But what's not impossible is making sure that your relationships are established early on and that they are honest and predictable. Remember that those two components to a relationship have nothing whatsoever to do with disability. Although far too often missing, they are the basis for all strong and long-term relationships.

Remember the high school student Pamela's story mentioned earlier in this book? It seemed apparent that what she wanted from her teacher was a trusting and honest relationship. Ultimately, Pamela and her teacher worked through what appeared to be insurmountable issues. Pamela was making good choices and excellent decisions for the betterment of her life. What more can you ask for? What was the difference that promoted change from Pamela? Was it the severity, duration, and frequency of the consequences? Was it the generosity and power of the rewards? Or was it the first time in Pamela's school life when someone said, "I like you no matter what."?

Probably the most gripping reality regarding relationships is that they can be based on honesty and predictability, or they can be based on fear, unpredictability, and coercion.

Ellen's past schooling was filled with interactions that taught mistrust. When she first entered high school, she had acute anxiety, the kind that accompanies unpredictability and dishonesty. In order to get started with Ellen in high school, we first had to establish a supporting relationship that would be the basis for whatever we did on campus.

The real tragedy is that Ellen is not alone in the world of mistrust. We must build new trusting relationships on hard work and sincerity. Without a trusting relationship between the teacher and the individual, we have only coercion and manipulation.

So what constitutes your relationship with the individuals you serve? Do they know you will punish them for misbehaving? Is that the basis for your relationships? Or is your relationship one based on trust?

Movement Disorders

Anne Donnellan and Martha Leary have spent the past decade looking at how movement is affected by having a disability. This is an important concern as we create a path for change.

Our first exposure to a movement difference came when facilitated communication provided an outlet for many people with autism. I have met many people whose thought processes are far beyond their ability to make their bodies perform. Some people simply cannot tell their body to perform a task and be assured their body will follow through. They cannot physically create the same outcome without someone supporting their motor movements from letter to letter on the keyboard.

Similarly, one of my current students moves differently than all the other kids in my classroom. For him, the twenty foot stroll to the classroom door might contain two or three full 360 degree turns. He might sit down to breakfast, but it might take him thirty minutes or longer to initiate eating the meal.

Obviously, motor differences are only one way we might explain his not eating. Some believe some individuals are simply unable to start the process of eating, so weight loss becomes profound and medically dangerous. Anne and Martha have identified some areas of motor difficulties. They include when individuals:

- do not respond (verbally or physically) as quickly
- do not switch activities or thoughts smoothly
- engage in repetitive movements to maintain their harmony
- do not appear to be trying to complete an assigned task.

In other words, they might be saying, "I simply cannot make my body do what I want it to do."

Instead of reading an individual's behavior, such as spinning on the way to the door, as volitional and intentional, think seriously of its possible connection to motor differences. That is a tough lesson for us – the educators – to understand. We feel proficient in movement and we work with many individuals who appear to be able to make their bodies work well. But we must understand that some people's bodies do not work in harmony with their thought processes. We should consider movement differences in all communicative intent list-making so that we do not omit a real possibility for some individuals.

Teaching Never Stops;
Learning Is Always Happening

It is imperative to remember that even in the absence of teaching, individuals learn. When I watch the individuals in my classroom, I am convinced that most of their learning happens outside our classroom and probably without a teacher. So in this arena, I am most concerned with the outcomes of bad instruction or the lack of teaching.

Contrary to the often formula-driven curricula and programs offered to the field of special education, vocational services, independent living, and supported employment, we need to be creative. I have always questioned why those of us who profess to serve the full range of individuals with disabilities are convinced that we should turn over all our thinking needs to the group of people who create the curricula, the statutes, the guidelines, the laws, the regulations, and the programs.

Before we attempt to teach new skill areas, we need to process and reprocess the materials, the need to learn, the setting, the need to teach, and the desired outcome. If we do not do that for people who already struggle to learn, we will not make it to the end of tunnel.

Poorly thought out processes rarely work and can have devastating effects on the learners. After eight years of experiencing little education, Dennis had learned to waste his time well. He also had learned to have no expectations for the day. So what did it mean when Dennis arrived in high school? Dennis was suspicious of everything and everyone because he did not know what instruction looked like. He fought his teachers about everything. He appeared unwilling to be productive while, in honesty, he had no idea what being productive on a daily basis meant.

While others had failed to teach him, Dennis had continued to learn. Instead of learning about knowledge and teaching, he had learned about wasting time. He could spend literally hours doing next to nothing. Wasting time is a very hard skill to acquire and maintain. But it is the primary by-product of attending school without any instruction or attending a sheltered workshop without any jobs to complete.

So while we might utter, "I never got the time to take Dennis to get a real job and support him there," what we should be admitting is "I inadvertently taught Dennis to fill up his own time." High school was a very interesting contrast from what Dennis and Ellen had learned in their previous eight years of schooling. As mentioned, Dennis had mastered the art of killing time without really doing anything. Ellen was totally anxious about everything and could not manage a single moment without being involved in something – hopefully something predictable.

In contrast to Dennis, Ellen's roller coaster ride in her first eight years of school had taught her to make things happen if others wouldn't and to have the last say so as to maintain whatever control there was. The real tragedy is that no one specifically sat down to teach neither Dennis nor Ellen the skills they acquired. What they learned just happened as the result of what did not happen.

I oftentimes hear parents talk about their typical kids having a poor teacher in second grade, but they had a great first grade teacher and might get a dynamite third grade teacher. They accept the ups and downs because they know most children will bounce back or recover from a year with a not-so-great teacher. On the other hand, individuals with disabilities can get trapped in unacceptable situations for many, many years. It is that dynamic that causes such harm.

In another situation in the late 1980s, there was a scandal in the Columbus, Ohio, public schools regarding the use of refrigerator boxes for timeout rooms. Without debating the ethics of timeout or the size of the refrigerator box, the issue in Columbus was the over representation of African-American individuals in those boxes. I would profess that those individuals may not have been learning to behave. But they were probably learning how bad they were as individuals and as a group, and how unfair the adults seemed to be toward themselves and their friends.

Every time you make a list of possibilities for communicative intent, keep in mind what that individual might have learned about his or herself as others have failed to provide adequate support or education. When we ask individuals to raise their hands before talking, we are hoping to teach order and fairness. But, we must also ask ourselves, "What does an individual learn who is not called on in the same way as other individuals?" I would hope you have a possible answer that might find its ways to a list someday.

Teaching Being vs. Doing

In David Hindsburger's book, *do? be? do?*, he creates a most interesting dilemma for providers. We need to remember that many times individuals need to learn how to be rather than how to do. I think the notion that there exists a fundamental difference in learning "to be" rather than "to do" creates a very intriguing and intellectually provocative topic for us to consider and solve for each individual we serve.

Questions always will exist in our field that require serious thinking and rethinking so that we, the educators, fully understand the implications for the people we serve. Throughout my many years working in the field of disabilities, I have loved the challenges that require me to think the most. The *do? be? do?* question is an important way of seeing those we serve as well as making intellectually sound decisions for what, where, and when we teach a particular skill. For example, professionals often see an individual as needing to learn to do things – counting, writing, reading, etc. But the individual never gets into difficulty because she can't do counting. It's because she struggles with being patient with others or with being able to help her teacher understand her issues. IEP and IPP objectives typically target all the doing skills and omit the being skills.

For individuals who lack good interpersonal skills, what is most important for them to learn? Why do we assume their interpersonal skills will improve if they are able to add and subtract, wash their hands, do pre-vocational skills, or state the letters of the alphabet? Individuals become more competent humans when they have skills for coping with difficult situations. They learn those skills only when someone specifically sets out to teach those skills.

Don't Blame the Individual for Not Having the Needed Skills

Recently, I testified on behalf of a fourth grade boy. It was clear that his behavior plan was based on his alleged unwillingness to use required skills. There was nothing in the observational data, behavioral analysis, or plan that even hinted at the possibility that the boy did not have the ability to perform the skills. So the entire premise of the plan hinged on the notion that if the boy would perform certain skills, he could earn tokens for good behavior. Specifically, if he was able to have patience, compassion, and tolerance for other children, he could earn tokens worth something at school. Of course, his behaviors in question were fighting, intolerance, and impatience. So if he was to be successful, he would need to use skills he did not have.

It is not unusual to see people act before they think. But it often results in some degree of disruption and disharmony. But what do we tend to do in these situations? In most cases we write some sort of behavior plan that asks the person to stop and step away from the situation before he or she acts. This always sounds great to the writer of the goal or plan. But if the person could stop before acting, he or she would. Simply formalizing the need or lack of awareness or skills by writing a plan or a goal does not create skills in the individual.

Skills are learned and taught in a dynamic situation. Before someone can stop and step back, he or she must see what is coming. Without the awareness of what's coming, the person always will be reacting to the situation. He or she is never in front of the problem, analyzing and problem solving. But if the plan provides rewards for good analysis and problem solving before the person knows how to see what's coming, the individual will not earn many rewards.

Dennis, who we met back in Chapter Two and again on page 41, had many previous negative learning experiences and he resisted new situations. In high school, we started with a doing skill he already had when we designed all his vocational activities. In that manner, we were trying to teach new being skills – waiting, trying hard, taking risks, and hoping things will be good for everyone.

To have chosen a task that required a doing skill when it was obvious he did not have the being skills would have been problematic. That strategy would have been fundamentally damaging to Dennis' learning and our relationship. This is a good example, because it honestly blends the doing vs. being issues with the question of having the needed skills.

Another good example comes from the issue of movement dysfunction. Just as with the individual who lacks the skills, someone impacted by the inability to perform a skill due to a movement disorder should not be behaviorally modified into moving more smoothly, transitioning more directly, thinking more quickly, or answering within five seconds.

So as we consider an individual's failure to have patience with peers, write his or her name, step away from a confrontation, wait for the city bus, or understand why there's no outing because it's Monday, we need to include on the communicative intent lists that maybe the person doesn't have the skills needed to perform the behaviors. And if people lack the skills, we should not expect them to excel if we fail to teach the necessary skills. In these situations, behavior modification is weak in comparison to strong teaching.

Become a Behavioral Educationalist

For the past eight years, I have called myself a behavioral educationalist knowing that such a term is meaningless to the majority of behavioral scientists. Regardless, I know what it means in my work. It revolves around an alternative approach to behavior change – viewing behavior as communication and acting as a change agent through teaching.

Replacement behaviors generally are not lying dormant waiting for a little watering. They are skills that require creative teaching on your part. Behavioral educationalists seek to understand another's behavior. They realize that the solution requires well-designed and well-executed teaching. Once again, we are making a clear distinction from one who sees the need for the individual to change prior to any change from the teacher or staff.

As a behavioral educationalist, you make the initial change. You take what you have learned about communicative intent and apply it to the design and focus of a teaching plan. Who changes first and whether we are gearing up to teach are important distinctions for this process and the success of everyone.

For example, Katie sometimes got upset. Going for a walk would help her to calm down. But a particular staff person would go for a walk with her only if Katie was truly doing well. The staff person was stating her position on the "continuum" of change. Her refusal clearly strengthened her position as one who believes that it is Katie's responsibility to change her behavior. She is unwilling to use the walk as a calming and regrouping activity for Katie. The walk is available only when there has been no upset behavior, no yelling and screaming, no throwing things, no hurting others. In other words, this staff person refuses to offer the walk as a strategy for healing and redemption.

This view of the walk narrowly defines the way this staff person sees both Katie and accommodating her challenges. But from what I understand from the dynamics, it is not a mystery at all. This staff person sees the walk as "reinforcing" and will not provide a reinforcing experience following a period of upset behavior. That would be reinforcing an unwanted behavior with an enjoyable activity.

Given that possibility, the staff person says, "NO!" For far too many of us, the issue is just that simple, just that behavioral, just that limited, just that narrow, and just that limiting.

But this can no longer be acceptable if we are willing to take an educational view of the problem. Presented with the information that the walk might be a way for Katie to recover from being extremely upset or a way for her to head off an episode of being upset and angry, the notion you would refuse the request to accompany Katie is completely contradictory to the desired outcome.

As a behavioral educationalist, you would seize the opportunity to teach Katie the power of her request and the excitement we feel that she is looking for a way to make amends, to improve her attitude, to seek a quieter place to relax, and to allow herself to be counseled and consoled. On the other hand, as a strict behaviorist, you would avoid engaging in any preferred activities with Katie until she was able to remain calm and upset-free. If we are honest in our interpretation of Katie's communicative message, we have to find an educational solution, not a behavioral morass, to define our goals for change.

Expect Individuals to Act Differently in Community and School/Program Settings

I cannot count the number of times professionals have blamed an individual's home life for his or her poor attainment in school or in an adult program. I fully understand why we feel the need to do this, but I do not think it helps anyone when we blame the parents or the individual.

Asking others to enter our public schools or jobsites with the expectation they will act differently, think wiser, work harder, and be kinder is the only way to proceed.

Let me give you an example: Let's say you have an individual who comes from a home where she has to be tough. When she arrives at school or work, she carries that toughness into that setting and things don't go right for her. She gets labeled and targeted for punishment for her tough behavior. What seemed a great strategy to the person – carry that toughness wherever you go – does not fit in this social framework of her school or job.

To help, we have to be incredibly creative and concrete. Before we jump into the outcome, let's take some time to analyze the situation from her perspective and from ours. Her need to be tough at home sets the frame for her thinking. When facing a different social dynamic, she needs to be able to answers question like these. "Will I need to be tough in the new setting and how can I judge that?" or "Who will I be without my toughness?" or "What will I do with my toughness when I enter the new setting?"

As an individual, facing these questions and finding answers might be easy or near impossible. The whole situation could require great levels of support just to answer the questions. But, we should know without even questioning ourselves that it is unfair to expect the person to stop being tough in all situations, because he or she will need it at home and possibly other places.

So, the sheer idea of punishing someone for being tough in the right situation and not knowing how to change that façade in a new setting makes no sense. Nothing is taught through this form of behaviorism except for what the person learns about us. So we have to decide that this situation is indeed serious and worthy of analysis and design.

Let's say this person is starting a new job, and we want to teach her that it is OK to leave her toughness at the door. Maybe you could create a special place in her locker where she physically removes her toughness shield and hangs it on the hook for the day. Maybe you could put a reminder – a sundial, a flower calendar, a potted plant – at her workstation to represent her new work persona: gentle. Then she is given permission to become that gentle person for the day. Just before leaving, she takes her toughness shield off the hook and puts it back on for use at home. This might explain how individuals might symbolically remove the shield they need at home until it is needed again. This explanation also might help the person see that the toughness shield is not needed at the job. Once she is able to remove the shield for the day, she will be able to experience the kindness and cooperation of her co-workers.

You could accomplish the same goal by providing a symbolically uplifting or gentle piece of clothing to wear, such as a T-shirt with a peaceful scene on the front. There are many people who walk into our social settings – schools, jobs, and community – leaving their home persona at the door. Once again, this is not an issue of disability. It is a very normal part of life for everyone.

We all create personalities for different occasions that we interchange frequently throughout the day. It works extremely well for most of us. But there are always people who will need extra help changing their approaches and understanding why it is important. For them, whether they have disabilities or not, we need to be prepared to teach them how and when. As teachers, we always should expect that we will support learning throughout the process. Whatever might be learned through punishment is not the outcome we are seeking.

Work with Vision in Search of Creativity

Don't allow yourself to be drawn into the trap of acting as a robot following the guidelines of a behavior plan written by someone who has no relationship with the individual. We should never relinquish our goal to be as creative in our teaching as is possible.

Many of the identified solutions or interventions in this chapter would not exist without creativity and an open-minded interpretation of the individual's actions. Simplistic behavior modification is really a boring approach to understanding and supporting others. With all the possibilities for seeing behavior as communicative, we cannot default back to a formula-driven approach to change.

Traditional behavior sciences would have us finding rewards and consequences for inappropriate behavior. We would initially spend most of our time establishing a menu of rewards and losses. Once we managed to establish our menu, we would then set up the terms and conditions for individuals' rewards and losses based on the presence of their inappropriate behavior.

Just look at the language that we create when we speak behaviorally. Our language loses all personal statements and identity as it becomes impersonal and generic. When language gets this generic, so does the intervention.

When we apply traditional behavioral sciences to human habits and actions, we can depersonalize the process to an extreme. Instead, we encourage the adoption of a new process, communicative intent, which should never be used to create generic interventions, depersonalize the individual, or limit anyone's creativity. Above all, keep your mind open and your ideas refreshed with what you know about the individual. Don't dilute the personal nature of your supportive interventions.

Behavior Modification Requires Adult Compliance

Within the system that is set up to monitor inappropriate behavior, we consistently have individuals who move from classroom to classroom or job to job or group home to group home without efforts to promote behavior change. It is always curious why very needy individuals are spared positive support plans even though the need is clear to everyone.

In establishing a positive support plan, it is important to maintain a consistent flow to our actions. For that reason, adult behaviors should be outlined and defined tightly. Well-constructed behavior plans detail what the trainer must do if the individual does ___. It is important to follow the plan so that we are able to promote the change it seeks.

Thus, any formal behavior plan is a document that monitors and controls caregiver, job coach, and teacher behaviors. Most interestingly, the vast majority of adults do not want their behavior governed by a plan. The notion of behavior plans seems quite appealing to most in the field as long as it is for someone else.

This is one of the primary reasons you find needy individuals without plans. Our resistance comes from the fundamental belief that plans are not for us, they are for them – whoever they may be. We are not in need of a plan; they are. It is about who's in charge and who needs to change. The idea that the plan would set in motion changes in our behavior is, on the other hand, not appealing to us. But that is the purpose of behavior plans – to establish a rhythm between individuals that is predictable and consistent over time, setting, and individuals.

Here lies the root of our resistance to really establish a narrowly defined response to another's behavior. We talk about the need to be consistent, but we struggle throughout the process to maintain even the shadow of consistency. We vehemently object to having our words and actions defined by a plan. We can no longer be ourselves because we are allowed to be only the person defined in the plan. From both a flexibility and consistency point of view, we, the teachers, caregivers, and job coaches, are not willing to give away that much to a plan.

It is always fascinating to see how people stretch and fudge on a plan that dictates their behavior. But in the same breath of protest, we would insist that the people we support need to follow the plan in all its positives and negatives because they truly need to change. The staff person who unilaterally decided that she did not have to go for a walk with Katie did so because she would not have to relinquish her beliefs and prejudices about Katie, her behaviors, and the plan.

So instead of plan compliance, we see maverick moves by the staff and caregivers. That is one of the fallacies about behavior plans and why most adults avoid them like the plague. There are better ways to avoid that control over your behavior – simply use the processes outlined in this book. There is nothing limiting and controlling about seeing another's behavior as communication and acting on that belief.

Let's consider Ellen and her game playing. If you follow the formal plan, you would have to seek remediation through the actions outlined for you, including ignoring, washing hands, and stating apologies. Your actions would be limited, but if you were to choose the alternative route, communicative intent, your actions would be geared to teaching more games and being more attracted to Ellen's game playing. How you create more games and playful interactions with Ellen would be based on your personality, strengths, and relationship with Ellen.

But more important than anything else, following the communicative intent process does not endanger or jeopardize your relationship with the person you are supporting. Seeing another's actions as communicative brings you closer to the individual. Whatever responses you undertake come about only after listening to that person.

Listening is one of the best equalizers for a relationship. Communicative intent makes a better and wiser choice for both of you.

CHAPTER SIX
◆◆◆

Confronting the Use of Punishment

We have explored the belief that communicative intent provides a better place to start any conversation regarding the actions of another person. Thus far, I have deliberately excluded punishment in the discussion of interventions.

The use of punishment is a questionable means to support the relationship you have worked to establish and maintain with another individual. This section will try to unveil the myths about punishment as a teaching tool. More broadly, it is a continuation of the unmasking of behaviorism and behavior management. There are fundamental differences between the framework of relationship building and traditional behavior management, both in their chosen strategies and their unique connections to individuals.

There are several concerns in the literature regarding the use of punishment.

Questionable Long-Term Effect on Behavior

Research shows without question that, in the long-term, punishment is not a fix of another's actions. Consider when parents discuss the behavior of children. Once the hammer has come down on the child and he or she is feeling the discomfort of the intervention, parents often report that "things are better and the original behavior has decreased."

But in the next breath and video, the parents are talking about what new problems have cropped up and are asking, "What do we do now?" The message expressed with the original behavior remains unheard. The child continues to express him or herself, now through more complex behaviors such as lying and directing anger at more defenseless members of the family.

All this happens because punishment typically applies a temporary patch, deafening the communication, only to have the message emerge in the form of another behavior. Dealing only with the communication or addressing the message will not completely satisfy the individual whose actions we dislike. The long-term impact we want will come only from listening to the communication and designing interventions that match the individual's messages.

Questionable Teaching Outcomes

An important consideration is the instruction and outcomes that precede the design and implementation of a behavioral strategy. This is where we might see the greatest discrepancy between what we profess we were doing and what the learning outcome is for the individual with behavioral challenges.

In our society, disobedience while driving is a rampant problem. To address this, we have applied punishment for offenders who are caught "red-handed." There appears to be a clear misalignment in our goal to reduce driving disobedience and to promote safer highways. Despite the claim that we are promoting the reduction of driving disobedience through financial loss to the offender, disobedience remains rampant.

Our daughter, Jessica, was killed in 1999 as a passenger in a car going twenty-five mph over the speed limit. The young woman driving had received a speeding ticket only nine days earlier. The intended behavior change prompted by the issuance of the speeding ticket had not saved Jessica's life. It failed in all accounts.

But probably the most detrimental effects of using punishment as a change agent are the misaligned teaching outcomes. For with speeding and other driving disobedience, most offenders actually have learned to be more vigilant, more alert, and more focused on devices to detect the "enemy," the police. So instead of teaching to slow down, the system has taught drivers to avoid detection and to be disobedient only when there is an absence of authority.

It has become a game – drive however you desire, but keep your eyes and radar detector on high alert. There is nothing satisfying about this instructional outcome, but it is a reality in our society.

Not only did this punishment scheme not protect Jessica, it also endangers all drivers. We have been taught to believe in the safety net created to protect us from driving offenders. This is a façade of protection that puts all of us at risk.

It is vitally important to understand that we, as a society, are expected to feel safer and protected by punitive measures that simply do not teach to the need, highway safety. Similarly, when individual are punished for one act or an array of acts, we might be actively teaching them to be deceitful, secretive, or untrustworthy, rather than teaching them to stop the undesired actions. When we design consequences for another's action, we must be truthful about what our intervention teaches and be prepared to tackle yet another array of actions that were caused by the choice to punish without listening.

Punishment Is Derived from a Superficial Understanding of the Individual

A paramount understanding in the use of punishment is the generic nature of the consequences. You can look at pretty much any societal punitive system and find a generalized approach to the consequences. In most cases, it is a take-away system that costs money or removes personal freedoms. Any personal or individual application of punishment is usually only in the amount of money or the length of the loss of personal freedom.

As with societal systems for punishing the actions of others, most punitive systems within group homes, sheltered workshops, day programs, and schools are generic in nature. They rely only superficially on the unique characteristics of an individual. For the most part, we need only gather information regarding an individual's dislikes and likes so that we can match up the takeaways.

In this book we have discussed linking relationships with successful learning and teaching. We should not abandon the need for a relationship for the simplistic perspective, "I only need to know what an individual doesn't want withheld or taken away." But, the simplistic nature of punishment is appealing for the person who is unable or unwilling to make a commitment to an individual. There is something almost addicting about the simplicity of punishing people for their actions.

But don't expect a great return from punishing others with generic consequences. It will not have the impact you expect. If you do not have a relationship with the individual posing problems, you have access to very few tools for promoting change. It is the chicken or egg analogy. Do we seek out punishment because we lack a relationship or do we use punishment to avoid establishing a relationship? Either way, it will not provide the relief you are seeking Avoid it at all costs.

Punishment Is an Intervention Only after the Action Has Happened

Punishment applies an unpleasant consequence following an action. We do not punish people unless they commit an act that is undesirable. Given the timing of the delivery of the punishment, we are not focused on anything but the committed action. In other words, punishment is entirely reactive.

If you are a deliverer of punishment, you will lock yourself into the role of waiting and then applying the consequence. All the systems our society has in place to deal with offending are focused on penalizing an individual for a breach of laws or rules. It is the accepted means for dealing with offenses against society. Despite its somewhat global acceptance, there are alternatives. Communicative intent provides a contrasting framework that relies on listening to messages embedded in another's actions and constructing solutions based on a commitment to the individual, not technology or science.

Punishment Does Not Expand Thinking or Help Us Create the Right Connection for the Individual

To act on little knowledge of an individual in search of a generic intervention that has been used on thousands of others should not excite us at all. As a professional, I find this reality the most limiting aspect of punishment. As we turn our efforts into making the best things happen for the people who need the most, we cannot use an intellectual vacuum as our staging point. That is totally unfair to the individual with challenges.

In schools, more and more of the curricula calls for a rote application of the lessons. There is a belief that learning is slowed by educators who create their own lessons and activities. Likewise, group homes are plagued by reams of plans that are to be followed, not challenged. Even if the staff person knows the individual affected by the plan much more intimately, they are not to vary from the plan.

We hold consistency as paramount to a successful behavior plan. The limiting power of the behavioral sciences directly contradicts this book's focus – communicative intent. In contrast to the minimalist thinking involved in deriving punitive consequences, using communicative intent as the framework for change requires synthesizing all the information we can gather as we design teaching interventions, not punishment.

Some People See Punishment as Payment

In *A Framework for Understanding Poverty* (2001), Ruby Payne discusses the impact of poverty on individuals and groups. The book defines poverty broadly, including financial, emotional, mental, spiritual, and physical, as well as others. But the most applicable part of this research for us is her revelation that not all people see punishment as linked to changing one's behavior.

Most remarkable are the people who see punishment as requiring only a payment for their wrong. They do not see punishment as a change agent. On the contrary, once they have paid their fine, they feel free to commit the action again. They are free of responsibility once they have paid the price.

This is a clash of cultures that we must try to understand. Once again, this stark contrast in how different groups see punishment demonstrates another limiting aspect of behaviorism. This research is provocative as well as critical to our understanding the clear limitations of using behavior management as our tool of choice.

Our challenge is to teach without the "sting" of punishment. As a teacher, I find this notion quite fascinating and satisfying. Once we have set aside the framework of behaviorism and punishment, we truly are forced to make positive sense of another's actions in order to design a teaching intervention.

Teaching without the "sting" implies that we see an individual's actions as meaningful, and worth our attention and understanding. In Herb Lovett's book, *Learning to Listen*, he describes working on behalf of others without the inclination to use punishment. This enables you to listen to and dream with the individual whose actions are in question.

When we say, "No," to punishment, the clouds of science and mythology are lifted. We have a chance to make decisions based on an individual's dreams, not their likes and dislikes. Is it possible that more of us can reach that place where we turn mythology into possibilities? Can we turn consistency into intimacy? Are we able to turn punishment into effective teaching? Can we turn knowledge into a relationship?

CHAPTER SEVEN

◆◆◆

The End of a Book,
the Beginning of a Process

In many ways, I never thought I would be writing the concluding chapter to a book that has allowed me to take the time to think about the years I have spent as a behavioral educationalist. It also has been a time where I got to think back over the years about the hundreds of children and adults with disabilities whose lives became intertwined with mine.

For many of my early years in special education, I was not drawn to these relationships as I am today. That closeness came when I met Mary, my partner. It was her relationships with children in special education that taught me the value of getting close and investing your soul. It is because of Mary that I have stories to tell that resonate the right way to teach.

I have tried my best to include some very personal stories that illuminate our need, as trainers or educators, to seek out new processes for promoting positive change. Through those same stories, I have tried to capture the predicaments in which many of the individuals we teach and serve find themselves. As a writer and an educator, I think that this process will be challenging for the best of us and impossible for many of us.

Seeing others as "broken" has been the foundation of special education and disability services. That is the way many of us have thought for decades. Consequently, it will be very hard for some to make the transition. On the other hand, I feel that as each of you struggle to change, you will learn things that I have not been fortunate enough to discover. Discovery in the face of human relationships is what makes the journey worthwhile.

Allow me to step back into the processes for just a moment. I would like to address, very specifically, the teachers and professional staff who have read this book. It was my intention to make this book both helpful and friendly to both you and the families of those you support and teach. Having said that, it is very important that you not forget the position many people are in as the parents of a individual with significant behavioral issues. Sometimes, we have a tendency to make these parents into the "bad guys" even when we know that type of labeling is of no value to anyone.

Once again, we might find ourselves in the labeling mode because that has been the practice of education and human services for so long. Remember that parents are simply other humans who face incredible challenges throughout their life with their son or daughter. Seeing parents as incompetent and/or enabling does not create a relationship that flourishes and grows.

Parents who are unsure of how to help their son or daughter are probably trying their best. They just do not know how to see their child differently and do not know how to approach change in a new way. Expecting these parents to come up with new strategies and new approaches is not being fair.

When parents lack the skills we want them to use, it is totally unfair for us, as professionals, to hold onto those expectations. Instead, consider looking for the communicative intent of their actions. People who are stuck and do not know where to go will show that through their actions.

A classic example might help drive home this point. Over the years, I have heard countless professionals complain that a particular set of parents simply refused to try medication for their child. While we, as educators, saw medication as a good option for the child, the parents continued to establish roadblocks preventing a trial of medication. If we were to step back and consider the following, we might be able to face the situation with honesty and concern:

Behavior: Refuse to try medications for their child

Communicative Intent:
>The parents don't have a doctor they can trust.
>The parents have no access to medical treatment.
>The parents have known others with "drug" problems.
>The parents have an addiction problem.
>The parents have already tried medications for their child with no
>>success.
>The parents have a healthy distrust of our system.
>The parents have heard other parents tell horror stories.
>The parents are in denial that their child has problems.
>The parents want us to change first, them second, their child third.

The parents have read the "headline stories" about meds.

The parents have witnessed so many more changes than we have.

The parents have no one to consult for advice and counsel.

The parents are very isolated as a result of their child's issues.

Yes, the processes we have discussed in this book can be applied to all of us. And if you look at the actions of some of the people you support in this manner, you could make a choice of a possibility that determines your role as helper or educator.

As I have always professed, this process is a human one, not a disability one. Families also can view your actions in a similar manner. Then maybe they could determine the proper role they should play based on the intent of your actions.

It is a two-way street with lots of traffic. So take care when dealing with parents. When testifying recently on behalf of the fourth grader (page 62), I was both pleased and saddened. It was wonderful to see this boy's father smiling and nodding as I described his son. At the same time, it was extremely depressing that no one else had ever been able to describe his son in kind words. All I was saying was that his son did not have the skills the school was attributing to him and that he should not be blamed for his social errors while in school. This story tells me how little some parents need in order to believe in themselves, in their family members with disabilities, and in us.

We have traveled together through a process that I believe will help both students and adults in most situations. It is not a foreign process to most professionals. But it can be used to assist change for some of our most challenging students and adults. The process presented here offers a clear alternative to traditional behavior management and behavior modification.

We all must have a clear understanding of the difference between communicative intent and the behavioral mythology we are too accustomed to using. I hope that I have:

1) provided philosophical background
2) distinguished the process from traditional behavioral approaches
3) provided intellectual insight into moving from the list of possibilities to teaching strategies

4) elaborated on specific behavior in the Appendix to make your jobs
    easier.

If I have succeeded, I feel gratified in writing this text.

I also realize that I have written about my innermost passion. I could not have written a book without revealing myself. Teaching has been an extremely gratifying career for me. I am very lucky to have had so many opportunities to take risks.

My beliefs about teaching have made up the foundation of this book as well as my beliefs about humanity. And so I ask each and every one of you to honor your own passion and make good your efforts to use the process I have defined. Whenever an individual releases a process to others for use with other humans, there is a built-in chance that it will be used improperly. Some would say that Skinner and Pavlov gave us a process. Others might say they gave us a science. But regardless of their intent as givers, I feel we have undertaken to use their findings unwisely.

What is even more disturbing is that we tend to use a powerful technology most unwisely in special education and adult services on people who are vulnerable. We tend not to use the "behaviorally sciences" at home against the members of our families nor with strangers who have wrongly interacted with us. We have, historically, maintained an unhealthy relationship with the behavioral sciences when we are dealing with individuals with significant learning and behavioral challenges.

With this understanding, I ask that you use the processes outlined in this text to better the lives of individuals with disabilities, not worsen them. If we are willing to accept behavior as communication, we need to be ready to hear the messages embedded in the actions of another. All this process helps us do, within our relationship with an individual, is ask that the message be delivered in a clearer and gentler way.

We must continue to want to hear these messages, because we believe they are important to the person.

PROLOGUE
◆◆◆

Before I started writing, I asked many colleagues to volunteer as editors. Having a support group of my own has been a comforting place to be. Most recently at a conference, I was standing in the middle of the hallway looking about for friends. As I stood there gawking, I noticed a woman had dropped several sheets of paper from her conference program. I leaned over to be helpful and as I stood up, she said, "Oh, you' re Larry Douglass. I'm Susan Yuan. I am reading your book."

I was pleased I had been courteous at that precise moment to face someone who had been so helpful. We took the time to talk and Susan told the following story.

Susan was helping another parent deal with a situation for her child. Susan's adult son, Andreas, had accompanied her. Susan had promised to help this parent with a very difficult situation, when Andreas started getting agitated and demonstrating a great deal of distress. Susan felt she had committed her time to the benefit of the other parent and felt uneasy about stating Andreas' obvious need to leave the building. Other adults in the situation were becoming irritated with Andreas' actions and were voicing their disapproval of Susan's management of the situation.

As soon as Susan could complete her responsibilities to the other parent, she and Andreas left the building. Once outside, Susan started talking about having been in the building years before. Andreas was quick to acknowledge both her awareness and his mother's attempts to smooth the events of the day.

In their discussion, Susan talked about the previous event that had brought them to the building. It had been three years before when Andreas visited his father and sister there. Her son responded favorably to her remembering the events.

And then as if second nature, Susan asked her son, "Do you think your father and sister are still here? And do you think that I was going to prevent your seeing them?"

Andreas was quick to affirm her fears about his feelings. Susan reached over and hugged him as she explained that his father and sister had returned to the Far East just after that visit. She went on to say that she would never prevent her son from visiting with them.

After all the criticism of Andreas' behavior, Susan knew which direction to go. She truly believes in Andreas' efforts to communicate through his actions, and his message matched to a tee.

APPENDIX
◆◆◆

The following lists some possible communicative intent for some specific challenging behaviors.

Abusing Substances
I need attention.

I feel needy (emotional or physical).

I need to escape from my feelings or problems.

I need an affliction.

I need an excuse for my situation.

I have poor self-esteem.

I am inadequate and incompetent.

I've learned this at home.

I like the way it feels.

I need revenge.

I seek to punish those who I feel are responsible for my situation.

I need to assert my independence/autonomy.

I am easily addicted.

Acting Apathetically
I'm bored.

I'm depressed.

I'm stressed.

I have poor self-esteem.

I feel inadequate and incompetent.

I need to keep others at a distance or avoid interactions.

I have poor social skills.

I'm distrustful.

I have a substance-induced problem.

I'm sick/tired.

I have a lack of facial expression.

I have low affect.

Acting as a Victim
I lack social skills.

I need attention.

I don't know how to have a successful interaction.

I want revenge.

I lack good role models.

I have poor self-esteem.

I feel inadequate and incompetent.

I learned this at home.

I've been abused (verbally or physically).

I've lost something.

I'm always criticized.

I'm not successful in anything
I try.
I feel sibling rivalry.

Acting Cruelly

I learned this behavior.
I'm expressing my anger.
I feel powerless.
I need to exert power.
I want revenge.
I need to keep others at a dis-
tance or avoid interactions.
I have a lack of conscience.
I'm trying to improve or main-
tain my status.
I lack empathy.

Acting Dazed and Confused

I have a substance-induced prob-
lem.
I feel depressed.
I feel stressed.
I have processing difficulties; i.e.
learning disability, ADD.
I have a head injury.
I'm sick/unwell.
I'm tired/fatigued.
I have allergies.
I'm having a hormonal reaction.
I'm infatuated with someone/in
love.
I'm daydreaming/thinking about
something else.
I'm bored.

Acting Paranoid

I have a psychiatric disorder.
I feel threatened.
I have a poor understanding of
social cues.
I feel guilt (real or exaggerated).
I am overcome by worry.
I'm stressed.
I have poor self-esteem.
I have poor social skills.
I have a substance-induced prob-
lem.
I require a predictable environ-
ment.

Acting Passive-Aggressive

I want to control everybody/ev-
erything.
I want the other person to lose
control.
I want a reaction.
I lack the verbal skills to express
myself.
I learned this behavior at home.
I have deep-seated emotional
reasons I don't want to deal
with.

Acting Secretively

I feel powerful when no one
knows all about me.
I can do anti-social or bad things
without people knowing.
I'm afraid I'm not good enough.

My cultural values don't allow me to reveal things to a stranger (teacher or staff person).

I am protecting myself because I feel very limited.

I feel paranoid.

I am avoiding the disapproval of others.

I am gaining the approval of others.

I don't know how to stop.

Acting Sexually Inappropriate

I am sexually abused.

I watch explicit media.

I want social acceptance within a gang.

I watch friends or family sexual behavior.

I want attention.

I have poor self-esteem.

Acting Sexually Precocious

I don't know how to deal with my sexual development/hormones.

I have been sexually abused.

I have seen this behavior at home/on TV.

I want attention/love.

I want to experiment/compare.

Acting Withdrawn

I look different.

I act different.

I am physically and sexually abused.

I am aggressive toward others.

I am withdrawn and unresponsive with peers.

Affiliating with Gangs

I want to be accepted.

I want to belong.

I have fear of not belonging.

I need protection.

I need to be seen as cool.

If I have friends I belong.

I'm their kind of people.

I like to be in groups.

I like to be on the edge.

I like to live dangerously.

I want to defy the law.

I want to defy authority.

I want revenge.

I want power and control.

Arguing

I feel sibling rivalry.

I want to rebel.

I am mad at someone.

I have a different opinion.

I feel peer pressure.

I'm not accepted by others.

I'm not getting what I want because someone is being mean to me.

I feel resentment.
I feel I'm always right.
I need to delay something.
I only get my point across when I argue.

Attacking Physically

I am physically or sexually abused.
I am on drugs.
I have a psychiatric problem.
I want social acceptance within a gang.

Biting

I have an oral fixation/stimulation.
I'm cutting teeth.
I need a way to deal with anger, frustration, fear, being threatened.
I want attention.
I lack communication skills.
I need to exert power.
I seek revenge.
I have a desire to see other's reactions.
I have poor social skills.

Bragging

I need to feel important.
I have poor self-esteem/image.
I feel inadequate/incompetent.
I have poor social skills.
I need attention.

I'm better than everybody (over-confident).
I need to assert myself.

Bullying/Bossing

I learned this from someone.
I feel angry.
I use this as a way to deal with frustration, fear, threats.
I need a way of controlling.
I feel mean.
I'm trying to improve/maintain status in class.
I'm trying to mother, but I'm bossy instead.
I want to stay on top.
I have a self-esteem problem.
I have a lack of empathy.

Buying Friendship

I don't know how to develop/maintain a friendship.
I've learned to manipulate to get what I want.
I need to have power and control in relationships.
I have poor social skills.
I'm anti-social.

Clowning (Overly Dramatic)

I need attention/reinforcement.
I am trying to hide something.
I'm acting my developmental age.

I'm on a power trip.
I have the older child syndrome.
I have poor self-esteem.
I've learned this as a defense mechanism.
I'm bored.
I need to escape/avoid work.
I'm unsure of the appropriate way to act.
I have language delays.
I have a dramatic personality.
I'm shy.
I need to relieve anxiety.

Coddling Peers

I am not accepted by my peers.
I have low self-esteem.
I don't know other ways to relate to peers.
I feel power when I coddle.

Complaining of Physical Ailments (Somatic Complaints)

I have asthma.
I have an actual physical problem.
I need attention from parents/teachers.
I want to avoid work/escape interactions with others because it is threatening or I have poor social skills.
I am trying to be controlling.

I am hoping to be sent home.
I am depressed.
I have emotional stress.

Crying

I am unhappy/hurt emotionally.
I have a physical pain/problems.
I want attention.
I don't know what to do.
I am frustrated.
I have fears.
I feel angry.
I want to avoid work.
I want self-indulgence.
I want power/control.
I feel stress.
I lack verbal/social skills to express feelings.
I'm afraid.
I'm emotionally overloaded.
I have emotional problems.
I have poor self-esteem.
I feel inadequate and incompetent.
I have raging hormones.
I'm acting my developmental age.
I'm overwhelmed.
I'm hungry.

Daydreaming

I need sleep.
I'm too warm/cold.
I'm excited about something.
I'm on medication.

I'm bothered by extraneous stimuli.

I need to relieve pressures of life.

I have emotional/family problems.

I have vision/hearing problems.

I need an out from what's happening.

I just ate.

Defying (Malicious or Assertive)

I have a problem with authority.

I don't know how to do assignment.

I avoid/delay.

I feel someone is taking advantage of me.

I feel insecure about my ability to do it.

I'm upholding my beliefs.

I feel my point is justified-teacher is incorrect.

I want power/control.

I want peer recognition/social status.

I need attention.

I want to question authority.

I learned this behavior.

I feel fear.

I feel angry.

I have frustrations.

I'm questioning if you care/allegiance.

I need the last word.

I have poor self-esteem.

Demonstrating Poor Hygiene

I have poor self-esteem.

I feel inadequate and incompetent.

I don' know any better.

I need control and power.

I want to avoid people.

I'm depressed.

I may have a physiological problem.

I get up too late.

I need help.

I learned it at home.

I lack basic resources.

I feel no one cares about my needs or me.

Depending on Others

I have poor self-esteem.

I feel inadequate and incompetent.

I've learned this from my cultural experiences.

I don't know how to be become independent.

I only feel loved when I'm dependent.

I live in a dysfunctional family (my dependency fills a need of my parent).

I'm afraid to be independent.

I only feel complete when I'm dependent.

Destroying Property

I feel destructive.
I want attention.
I want to punish others.
I don't like the things.
I want revenge.
I don't see any consequences.
I don't care what others feel.
My attitude is "who cares?."
I overwhelmed by my emotions.
I don't know how to demonstrate my anger with words.
I have poor self-esteem.
I feel inadequate and incompetent.
I know I can't I can't hurt the person so I hurt their things.
I feel powerless.
I don't know how to get my family to deal with me.
I do it because it feels good.
I don't care about things.
I am stressed out and need a release.

Doodling

I'm bored because the lesson is too hard/too easy/too repetitive.
I enjoy the activity/I'm an artist.
I need it to keep me focused/awake.
I don't understand what's going on.
I need it to diffuse my energy.
I need to be engaged in something/it's all I can focus on.
I didn't know there was something to do.
I didn't realize I was doing it.
What's wrong with drawing, I'm paying attention.
I'm bored.
I can do several things at the same time.
I like to draw.
I'm listening.
I'm lost.
I need help.
I thought it was OK.
I need to keep my hands busy.
I don't care what is happening.

Eating Non-Food Items

I am anxious and/or worried.
I have a vitamin/mineral deficiency.
I can't screen out visual and auditory stimuli.
I have an emotional disturbance.
I want attention.

Exhibiting Eating Disorders (Over-Eating, Anorexia, Bulimia)

I want control.
I don't like myself.
I learned this behavior.
I am anxious and/or worried.
I can't deal with the reality of a situation.

I don't know any other way to deal with the intense feelings (fear, rejection, love, anger, etc.).
I want to punish someone.
I have Prader-Willie Syndrome.

Exhibiting Quick Temper

I can't read body changes.
I'm impulsive.
I can't relax.
I see patterns in routine.
I'm unpredictable.
I get response.
I get outcome.
I feel it works.
I see other people doing it.
I don't understand what is bad about being this way.
I don't see from others perspective.
I don't see the need to slow down.
My attitude is, "Why not?"
I feel it gets things resolved.

Exhibiting Regressive Behavior

I have a new sibling (expected/born).
I'm afraid.
I need attention.
I am insecure.
I'm going through changes in my environment.

I am moving to a new area/away.
I have physical or emotional problems.
I have changes in family configuration.
I'm reacting to trauma/uncertainty.

Exhibiting Shyness

I have low self-esteem.
I have low/no communication skills.
I'm afraid to be inadequate in front of others.
I'm an abused child.
I have a shy gene.
It is part of my culture.
I feel overwhelmed by my environment.
I'm afraid of others.
I feel depressed.
I'm schizoid.
I'm responding to something that has been done to me.
I feel insecure in certain situations.
I am dependent on others.
I have other psychological disorders.

Exhibiting Suicidal Behavior/Suicidal Ideation

I am depressed.

I am in an abusive situation.

I don't feel like I can go on living.

I have poor self-esteem.

I want to join a loved one who has died.

I can't see any way to change the situation.

I have a substance abuse problem.

I feel worthless.

I feel I have a problem with my sexuality.

I want to punish my family.

I want attention.

I want to shock people.

I need help.

Failing to Attend Regularly

I have to help my parents at home.

I have to stay home to be with my parents.

I am afraid/phobic.

I don't complete my homework.

I want attention.

I need my parents to focus on me so they won't focus on their problems with each other.

I am sick.

I am embarrassed.

I don't understand.

Failing to Bond

I've never learned how to bond.

Every time I try, I get burned.

I protect myself from abandonment.

My disability makes it difficult.

My adults don't model well.

I try, I fail.

I can't let myself get close.

Failing to Comply

I don't understand.

I'm rebelling.

I'm demonstrating a learned behavior.

I'm afraid.

I'm in puberty (hormonal changes).

I want everything my way.

I don't agree.

I want peer acceptance.

I'm engaging in a power struggle.

I want attention.

I'm acting out my values.

Failing to Be Prepared

I don't understand the task.

I don't have/own the materials.

I want to bug the teacher.

I need attention.

I'm unorganized.

I have other emotional factors
involved (peers/home).
I feel the need for avoidance.
I lack confidence in my ability.

I am defiant.
I am disorganized.
I want attention.
I am afraid.

Failing to Be Punctual

I want to be in control.
I don't know how to organize.
This is not important to me.
I want attention.
I don't like to wait; I want to get
started immediately.
I don't want to be there.
I don't feel wanted.
I have no assistance at home.
I am tired/ I have had inadequate
sleep.
I am responsible for other sib-
lings.
I have to rely on others to get to
school.
I like to disrupt class.
I am afraid to come to school.
I don't like school.

Failing to Be Responsible

I have low self-esteem.
I have low cognitive skills.
I am not organized.
I have no parental supervision.
I am on drugs.
I don't understand what's expect-
ed of me.
I don't understand the issue.
I don't think I own the problem.

Failing to Complete Tasks

I don't understand the task/
I think it's too complex.
My family imposes so much/
I don't have time.
I have poor self-esteem.
I lack materials.
I need more frequent reinforce-
ments.
I lack organizational skills.
I've learned this pattern, to never
finish.
I need attention.
I'm overwhelmed by the scope
and complexity of the task.
I don't have the skill.

Failing to Complete Work

I'm bored.
I lack discipline.
I lack focus.
I do not like the environment/I'm
distracted.
I lack motivation.
I've been abused (verbally or
emotionally).
It's too hard.
I don't understand.

Failing to Focus Auditorily

I am physically unwell.

I have a cold.

I can't hear properly.

My hearing aid distorts sound.

I hear other students making noise.

I hear outside noises that are competing with the instructor (lawnmower & airplane).

Failing to Focus Visually

I can't see well.

I have visual perceptual problems.

I am using drugs.

The room is poorly lighted.

The room layout prevents me from seeing the instructor.

Failing to Follow Directions

I think the directions are too hard/too repetitive.

I have language processing problems/I can't remember.

I have hearing problems.

I'm upset about emotional/family problems.

I don't want to/don't have to.

I'm experiencing peer pressure (I want to be cool).

Failing to Follow Routine/Schedule

I want power/attention.

I don't know/understand what is expected.

I have transition problems.

I get bored too easily.

I want to be contrary.

I need to escape/avoid.

I don't know the routine.

I don't want to comply.

I didn't set the routine.

I want to set my own pace.

Your routine is not important to me.

I'm always in trouble anyway.

I'm a rebel.

I get acceptance from my peers.

I thought I was on schedule.

Failing to Follow Rules

I have poor self-esteem.

I feel inadequate and incompetent.

I need attention.

I need control and power.

I don't understand and/or remember the rules.

I don't care about rules.

I need more help that I am getting.

I need stronger limits set for me.

I didn't make the rules.

I feel these rules are against my values/beliefs.

I don't agree with the rules.
I have no participation in making the rules.

Failing to Listen

I have hearing problems (acuity).
I have language problems (processing).
I have emotional/family problems.
I'm passive-aggressive.
I need attention.
I hear competing messages (can't filter).
I don't think it's important.
I don't know how to show respect.
I only hear yelling (I've learned to tune out).

Failing to Make Appropriate Eye Contact (Lack of or Staring)

I am shy.
I am a person with autism.
My cultural views on this are different.
I am unsure of the situation.
I have low self-esteem.
I am depressed.
I have a substance abuse problem.

I am showing aggression.
I am defiant.
I am self-stimming.

Failing to Pay Attention

I have hearing/vision problems.
I don't understand the task.
I have ADHD or ADD.
I have emotional/family problems.
I'm bored/the task is too easy/repetitive/too hard.
I am experiencing too many environmental distractions.
I can't tune things out.
I'm not sure what's important.
I don't understand.
I'm worried about other things.
I can't screen out visual and auditory stimuli.
I'm having hallucinations.
I'm too hot/cold/sleepy/hungry/sick.
I don't want to be here.
I'm medicated.
I have allergies/asthma.
I am having seizures.
I am more interested in my peers.
I need attention.

Failing to Respond

I'm angry.
I don't understand response expected.

I get power from not responding.
I have hearing problems.
I have emotional/family problems.
I'm electively mute.
I hate how I sound.
I have poor self-esteem.
I am depressed.
I am not attending.
I am developmentally delayed.
I am being defiant.
I have limited language skills.
I am ill.
I am using drugs.

Failing to Show Empathy

I don't care about others.
Others don't care about me.
I don't understand empathy.
I've never been taught to empathize.
I'm stronger than the others.
I think it's fakey.
I'm a loner.
I'm tough; how about others?
I'm the bully.

Failing to Show Remorse

It's not my fault.
I'm a victim of circumstance.
I've leaned to duck responsibility.
I don't understand how others feel.
I don't believe my behavior impacts others.

I'm responding as I've learned.
I don't understand what remorse is.
I am without a conscience.
I don't care about others.
Others don't care about me.
I'm the real victim here.

Failing to Stay Seated

I need to be moving.
I physically can't sit still.
I need to use the rest room.
I want to disrupt the class.
I need attention.
I don't understand the class schedule/routine.
I don't want to follow the schedule/routine.
I need assistance.
I cannot work independently.
I want to socialize.

Failing to Volunteer

I'm shy.
I have poor self-esteem.
I don't know information required.
I'm angry.
I'm insecure.
I'm lazy.
My culture doesn't volunteer.
I can't take a risk.
I've got nothing to gain.
I don't want to go against the social norm.

I get publicly anxious.
I'm bored.
I feel inadequate/incompetent.
I don't know the answers.
I have low cognitive skills.
I have low language skills.

Failing to Work in a Group

I feel shy.
I have poor social skills.
I am fearful of other children.
I am a perfectionist /I'd rather do it myself.
I don't like other kids.
I don't know how to wait my turn.
I get lost in a group.
I don't understand how the group works.
I want individual teaching.
I learn only by myself.
I'm embarrassed by my abilities or inabilities.
I loose too much in a group.
I get distracted too easily.
I feel bad when I don't perform well.
I have low self-esteem.
Nobody wants me in a group.

Fidgeting/Out of Seat

I'm bothered by environmental distractions.
I have ADHD.

I'm bored.
I need a way of focusing/need movement.
I have a poor diet.
I'm physically uncomfortable.
I have poor circulation.
I am taking medication.
I have a short attention span.
I am physically or sexually abused.
I have a physical problem (itch or pain).
I am not able to understand the lesson.
I am unwilling to cooperate with classroom routine.
I feel uncomfortable on this furniture.

Going Limp/Dropping

I am afraid.
I don't understand.
I have seizures.
I am sick.
I can't screen out visual and auditory stimuli.
I want attention.
I don't like this.
I don't want to be here.
I want control.

Hitting

I want attention.
I need a way to deal with anger, frustration, fear, being threatened.

I'm trying to make physical contact and am unaware of hurting people.

I'm trying to improve my social status.

I learned this from someone.

I feel this impulsive behavior.

I feel I must strike first due to perceived fear/weakness.

I am afraid.

I have poor social skills.

I have poor self-esteem.

I identify with aggressors.

Hoarding

I feel needy (emotional or physical).

I have Obsessive-Compulsive Disorder (OCD).

I need attention.

I need power.

I don't know how to share.

I feel sibling rivalry.

I never have anything.

I am afraid of losing something.

I lack security.

Ignoring

I want power.

I have learning problems.

I'm passive-aggressive.

I have a language problem/don't understand expected response.

I'm afraid of this person.

I don't want to accept the reality of a situation.

I don't understand.

I am afraid.

I can't screen out visual and auditory stimuli.

I feel superior.

I don't want to stop what I am doing.

I can't stop what I am doing.

I don't like you.

I don't know how to interact with others.

I want control.

Invading Personal Space of Others

I am trying to get attention.

I am unfamiliar with personal space mores.

I want physical contact.

I don't know how to initiate contact.

I want to start a confrontation.

I am exerting power over you.

Lying

I simply can't stop.

I'm trying to avoid someone's reaction to the truth.

I didn't know it was wrong.

Everyone lies to me.

Lying is easier.

I want to hide myself/my feelings.

I don't know the truth.

I get acceptance from others.
The truth is painful.
I'm in denial.
Once I've lied, I can't stop.
Others don't want to hear the
    truth.
It's my style of interaction with
    ____.
I am unaware of my lies.
I lie without even thinking.
It's a habit.
I want to look smart, not blank.
I want to manipulate others.
I have power over others.
I want to avoid a consequence,
    i.e. punishment, rejection.
I don't want to face a painful
    memory.
I don't understand.
I want attention.
I need to be in control/ I need
    power.
I learned this behavior.

Making Excessive Excuses
I learned this behavior.
I am afraid to fail.
I don't understand.
I want attention.
I don't want to do this now.
I think this is too hard.

Making Faces
I want attention.
I have poor social skills.

I need to avoid/delay.
I'm trying to gain power.
I want to make others feel bad.
I want to get a reaction.
I need to be overly dramatic.
I'm expressing my opinion.
I want to be silly or funny.
I'm trying to be theatrical.
I want to get a reaction.
I'm jealous.

Making Noises
I am a person with Tourette's
    Syndrome.
I'm bored.
I feel good/self stimulating.
I'm obnoxious.
I need to relieve tension.
I've learned this as a habit.
I want attention.
I am nervous.
I am obsessive-compulsive.
I am trying to distract others.
I am trying to disrupt the
    teacher.

Moving Incessantly
I don't have the correct medica-
    tion dosage.
I have a poor diet.
I haven't had demands to con-
    form before.
My body goes at this speed.
I didn't know I was different.

I simply do not know how to slow down.

I need medication.

I get lots of attention.

My body chemistry is beyond my control.

I see others moving quickly.

Picking (Excessive Personal Habits)

It's a habit.

I am insecure.

I need attention.

I need self-stimulation.

I need to relieve the physical pain.

I have sensory disorders.

Playing Alone

I'm unable to communicate.

I'm shunned by other children.

I have no interactive skills.

I really like this particular toy/activity.

I'm fearful of other children.

I find being alone comforting.

Refusing to Speak (Selective Mute)

I feel anger towards an adult.

I feel confused.

I don't understand the language presented to me.

I have a hard time forming thoughts into words.

I have a sore throat.

I have sore teeth.

I have sores on my tongue or mouth.

I need attention or sympathy.

I've had something very traumatic happen to me.

I want power.

Refusing to Take Turns

I need to be in control.

I have poor self-esteem.

I'm not ready to engage in reciprocal play.

I have poor social skills.

I feel inadequate and incompetent.

I want to avoid interactions with people.

I need attention.

I have no empathy.

Running Away

I need to get away from this situation.

I am afraid/phobic.

I don't understand.

I need to move around a lot.

I like how running feels.

I need attention.

I want to be in control.

Screaming

I need attention.

I'm trying to communicate feelings of: frustration, anger, fear, pain, discomfort.

I feel the need to avoid/delay.

I have a substance-induced problem.

I feel good when I scream.

Self-Isolating/Hiding

I am afraid.

I don't understand.

I feel superior.

I feel inferior.

I want attention.

I don't know how to interact with others.

I'm too hot/cold/sleepy/hungry/sick.

I can't screen out visual and auditory stimuli.

Self-Mutilating

I want attention.

I need a way to deal with emotional/physical pain.

I feel self-hatred.

I need self-stimulation.

I have an accidental/obsessive habit that goes too far (scratching).

I'm depressed.

I'm stressed.

I'm having a hormonal reaction.

I learned it in an institution where things are really crazy.

Sleeping

I did not get enough sleep.

My drugs/meds are affecting me.

I'm just bored.

I'm suffer from a nutritional deficit.

I ingested something other than food.

I'm overwhelmed, I want/need to escape.

I just ate a big meal.

I'm too hot/the room is too warm.

Speaking Inaudibly (Low Voice/Volume)

I have a physical pathology.

I have poor self-esteem.

I'm shy.

I learned this behavior.

I want attention.

I have a fear of failure.

I feel depressed.

I'm sick/tired.

I'm embarrassed by my voice.

I need to control.

I demand proximity.

Speaking Negatively about One's Self

I am a victim/I've been abused (verbal or physical).
I am insecure.
I feel awkward.
I lack self-confidence.
I have physical problems.
I need glasses.
I'm in grief.
I'm afraid.
I'm frustrated.
I feel things are my fault.
I feel neglected.
My basic needs are not met.
I have many problems that have not been cared for.

Speaking Out Inappropriately

I have an idea/I must tell someone.
I did not know it's not OK.
I don't get noticed.
If I don't talk out, I don't get to tell others
I am unaware of the system.
I have no storage system/I refuse to lose my ideas.
My ideas are very important to me.
Talking is my strength, my identity.
Writing and reading are my weaknesses.

I want to be known for my strengths.
Others talk when they want.
I can't predict being called on.
I need to be in control.
I want to disrupt.
I know how to "bug" the teacher or the boss.
I want others to respect/like me.
I want others to lose.
I want peer contact/attention.
I am simply defiant.
I don't like the rules.
I did not make the rules.
Following rules only works for certain people.
I want recognition for what I know.
It's my way of maintaining my self-esteem.

Spitting

I want attention.
I have something in my throat.
I learned this from someone (parent/sibling).
I use this as a way to deal with anger, frustration, fear, threats.
I am trying to humiliate someone.
I lack communication/social skills.
I feel the need to distance people.
I want power.
I want to avoid interactions.

I use this as a way to get peer/
    group recognition.
I'm good at spitting; otherwise
    I'm not good at most things.
I think it's a great game.

Stealing

I want it.
I need it.
I know stealing – it is I – I am it.
I live in a culture of stealing.
I want to impact another person.
I never get caught.
Others steal/why not me?
My friends steal.
Stealing gains me friends/status.
Stealing/being problematic is my
    identity.
I just borrowed it – you call it
    stealing.
Someone said I could have it.
Stealing creates my sense of
    worth.
Stealing makes my life OK.
I like taking risks.
I simply defy authority – stealing
    is only one-way.
I have been stealing for years
    – no big deal.
I didn't know it was wrong.
I don't think it hurts anyone.
Someone gave it to me.
Things stolen from me.
I need to stay out of trouble with
    ___.

I did it on a dare.
I need things to trade.

Stripping Clothing

I need attention.
I need to relieve stress.
I've been abused.
I'm demonstrating a learned
    behavior.
I have a sensory disorder.
I have emotional problems.
I am physically uncomfortable.
I am uncomfortable.
I don't care what others think.
I feel good when I strip.
I have emotional stress.
I don't understand the social
    standards.

Sulking and Pouting

I want to have things my own
    way.
I am spoiled.
I am bored.
I am frustrated.
I am on power trip.
I don't know to safely express
    myself.
I get attention.

Swearing

I'm mad.
I'm jealous.
I feel frustrated.
I'm upset.

I feel more important.

Peer pressure.

I feel societal influences to do this.

I hear it in the media/home a lot.

I need to relieve tension.

I need to make strong statements.

I can't express my feelings.

I am a person with Tourette's Syndrome.

I can really make my point.

Tantrums

I want to escape.

I want it gone.

I want a response to behavior.

I want attention.

I can't say, "No thanks."

I'm not heard when I speak quietly.

I want peer recognition.

I don't understand.

I'm confused.

I'm scared.

I'm afraid.

I want to delay.

I want to avoid.

I feel this is very effective.

I have poor communication skills.

I am not getting my way/needs met.

I'm not in control of my emotions/temper.

Tattling

I want attention.

I have low self-esteem.

I only know this way to interact.

I don't understand the social norms.

I can't interact appropriately with my peers.

I am trying to divert attention from myself or another problem.

Teasing

I need to be controlling/intimidating.

I don't understand social norms.

I want to interact even if it's inappropriate.

I only know how to interact this way.

I need attention.

I need power.

I want to build status.

I'm trying to divert attention.

I have poor self-esteem.

I have learned this from others copying others.

I lack empathy.

I feel social pressure.

I'm seeking revenge.

I'm jealous.

I feel cool when I do this.

I'm mad at someone.

I'm reacting to fear.

Threatening

I learned this as a way to get
what I want.

I identify with aggressors.

I need power/control.

I lack self-worth.

I need to delay perceived threat
or to avoid it.

I seek revenge.

I have poor social skills.

I want attention.

I have a substance-induced problem.

I need to gain social status.

I want to distance others.

I'm paranoid.

I get an outcome.

I feel it's very efficient.

Throwing

I want it gone.

I want a response to behavior.

I want attention.

I cannot say, "No thanks."

I'm not heard when I speak
quietly.

I want peer recognition.

I feel people don't care.

Touching Others Inappropriately

I want attention.

I don't know how to initiate
interaction.

I want to start a confrontation.

I want to see your reaction.

I want to get you in trouble.

I have been physically/sexually
abused.

I have learned this from my
siblings.

Using Rude/ Discourteous Language

I feel it's the way people talk.

I want to defy authority.

I want to get results.

I need attention.

I want to escape.

I want peer recognition.

I'm pushing buttons.

I don't see this as wrong; it's
normal to me.

Whining

I want attention.

I am depressed.

I have low self-esteem.

I have poor social skills.

I have learned this response/
habit.

I am trying to be irritating.

I am tired/sick.

Worrying Excessively

I have poor self-esteem.

I feel inadequate or incompetent.

I need to divert my thoughts to
delay something else.

I have anxiety about abuse.

I have anxiety about abandon-
    ment.
I have anxiety about basic needs
    being met.
I have an emotional problem.
I'm hyper-vigilant.
I'm neurotic.
I've got an obsessive-compulsive
    disorder.
I need attention.
I have family/personal problems.
I have unreasonable expectations
    from home.
I'm being threatened at school.
I've been abused or abandoned.
I'm a perfectionist.

BIBLIOGRAPHY
◆◆◆

Anne M. Donnellan and Martha R. Leary, *Movement Differences and Diversity in Autism/Mental Retardation: Appreciating and Accommodating People with Behavior and Communication Challenges*, Madison, WI: DRI Press, 1995

Anne M. Donnellan, Patricia L. Mirenda, Richard A. Mesaros and Lynette L. Fassbender, "Analyzing the Communicative Function of Aberrant Behavior," *JASH (now Research and Practice for Persons with Severe Disabilities),* Vol. 9, No. 3, pps. 201-212, 1984

V. Mark Durand and Daniel B. Crimmins, *The Motivation Assessment Scale (MAS): Administration Guide,* Topeka, Kansas: Monaco and Associates, 1992

David J. Hingsburger, *do? be? do?: What to Teach and How to Teach People with Developmental Disabilities*, Richmond Hill, Ontario: Diverse City Press, 1998

Herbert Lovett, *Learning to Listen: Positive Approaches and People with Difficult Behavior*, Baltimore: Paul H. Brookes Publishing Company, 1996

Ruby Payne, *A Framework for Understanding Poverty*, Highlands, TX: aha! Process, Inc., 2001

ABOUT THE AUTHOR
◆◆◆

Larry W. Douglass has over 30 years of experience as a behavioral specialist and educator throughout the United States. He is currently a special education teacher in the Highly Skilled Migrant Programme at Ridgeway Comprehensive School in Plymouth, England, supporting the mainstream education of teenagers with autism spectrum disorder (ASD). He is also a regular presenter at various behavioral conferences throughout the US, including TASH and Supported Life Institute.

Prior to publishing *Respectful Relationships and Effective Teaching*, he served as behavioral specialist and consultant to several educational institutions, including behavioral consultant for the Department of Education in California. He has extensive experience working directly with students, faculty, and families as well as service providers. Mr. Douglass also contributed a chapter on student behavior and learning disabilities to "I Can Learn," published by the California Department of Education.

Throughout his years of education and behavioral experience, his focus has been on providing a change to the science of behavior modification and helping service and education staff to view behavior as communication.